# A New Mexico
## Land Ethic Handbook

# A New Mexico
## Land Ethic Handbook

Richard L. Rubin
with
Andrew Gulliford and Leeanna Torres

NIGHTHAWK PRESS
TAOS, NEW MEXICO

A thoughtful and practical exploration of Aldo Leopold's Land Ethic, tracing its roots in the landscape of northern New Mexico and its ongoing relevance here in the place that first gave rise to it.
— Kristina G. Fisher, Past President, Albuquerque Wildlife Federation founded by Aldo Leopold.

Aldo Leopold expressed that his vision of a Land Ethic was the "end result of a life journey." This delightful and engaging *Handbook* shares information, insights, and inspiration gleaned from Richard, Leeanna, and Andrew's journeys. While Aldo Leopold's Land Ethic is often presented as a vision, or as an idea, it is truly an action- striving to live out the reality that we are all interconnected with each other and the land, water, and wildlife all around us. This New Mexico *Handbook* shares how three intentional, thoughtful, and eloquent individuals are trying to live their own land ethic.
— Wellington "Buddy" Huffaker, Executive Director, The Aldo Leopold Foundation, Baraboo, Wisconsin.

A deepening understanding of querencia informs these reflections on the ecological writing and activism of Aldo Leopold. The folk concept illuminates how multigenerational love of land and experience in place shapes the knowledge that science organizes and ethics tempers. The power of metaphor prepares us to read a watershed, to think like a mountain, and to imagine communities of flora and fauna as family. Aldo's love affair with New Mexico gave him the foundation for an exemplary career and the roadmap that led him into the wilderness. Richard Rubin offers an almanac of quotes from the teacher, the example of finding his own querencia in the valleys of Taos, and a useful catalog of Land Ethic institutions. Andrew Gulliford traces the extirpation of wolves and how that green fire in their eyes helped us understand them not as varmints but as a keystone species. With humor and compassion, Leeanna Torres explores her querencia, a family with ancestral attachment to the land who learned to survive and thrive upon it.
— Enrique Lamadrid, Querencias Series Editor, University of New Mexico Press.

*A New Mexico Land Ethic Handbook* is a thoughtful companion to the writings of conservationist Aldo Leopold. The authors share their Land Ethic experiences and personal observations, which are appropriately grounded by quotations from Leopold's landmark *A Sand County Almanac*. An inspiring read.
> — Joan Livingston, novelist and former The Taos News editor-in-chief.

About this world we're inhabiting: we need to talk. We need to listen. We need to come together. A New Mexico Land Ethic Handbook invites us to do just that, with Aldo Leopold's land ethic in our hearts and minds.
> — Laura Paskus, Leopold Writing Program Mi Casita resident; author, *At the Precipice: New Mexico's Changing Climate*.

In New Mexico it comes from the heart. Before that it comes from the land itself. We walk in reverence for this place we call home. Only recently have we discovered that it is called a "Land Ethic." Drawing that connection is the job of writers like Aldo Leopold, as appreciated today by Richard Rubin, Andy Gulliford, and Leeanna Torres, inspiring us to evolve in sacred reciprocity as guardians of Earth. The result is a deeply moving book and a beautiful gift to our community.
> — Roberta Salazar, Founder and Executive Director of Rivers and Birds, Arroyo Seco, New Mexico.

*A New Mexico Land Ethic Handbook.* Copyright © 2024 Richard Rubin. All rights reserved. No part of this publication may be reproduced, distributed, or transmitted in any form or by any means, including photocopying, recording, or other electronic or mechanical methods, without the prior written permission of the publisher, except in the case of brief quotations embodied in critical reviews and certain other noncommercial uses permitted by copyright law. For permission requests, write to the publisher, Attention Permissions Coordinator at Nighthawk Press, PO Box 1222, Taos NM 87571.

Foreword © Andrew Gulliford.

Chapter 6, Gila Wilderness Complexity © Andrew Gulliford.

Chapter 7, Our Wolf Ethic Inheritance © Andrew Gulliford.

Chapter 10, Exploring Querencia as a Land Ethic © Leeanna Torres.

Photos pages, 80, 85, 87, 90, 97 © Andrew Gulliford.

Illustration page 148 © Concepcion Torres.

Articles by Richard Rubin, reproduced courtesy Taos News.

Photo page 47, Aldo Leopold Shack, Baraboo Wisconsin. Courtesy Wonder al, CC BY-SA 3.0 <https://creativecommons.org/licenses/by-sa/3.0>, via Wikimedia Commons.

FIRST EDITION

2024

PRINTED IN THE UNITED STATES

ISBN: 979-8-9888976-2-0

Library of Congress Control Number: 2024943764

Authors: Richard Rubin, Andrew Gulliford, Leeanna Torres

Cover and book design: Kelly Pasholk, yourbookdesigned.com

Publisher: Nighthawk Press, nighthawkpress.com

*We dedicate the spirit and proceeds of this book
to the U.S. Forest Service and the
Friends of Mi Casita Fund
at the Taos Community Foundation.*

# Contents

Foreword by Andrew Gulliford . . . . . . . . . . . . . . ix
Introduction by Richard Rubin . . . . . . . . . . . . . . 1

1. The Land Ethic in Leopold's Words
   Richard Rubin. . . . . . . . . . . . . . . . . . . . . . . . 13
2. Selected Land Ethic Commentaries
   Richard Rubin. . . . . . . . . . . . . . . . . . . . . . . . 19
3. Land Ethic Origin and Evolution
   Richard Rubin. . . . . . . . . . . . . . . . . . . . . . . . 29
4. Today's Land Ethic Institutions
   Richard Rubin. . . . . . . . . . . . . . . . . . . . . . . . 45
5. Modern Wilderness Encounters
   Richard Rubin. . . . . . . . . . . . . . . . . . . . . . . . 57
6. Gila Wilderness Complexity
   Andrew Gulliford . . . . . . . . . . . . . . . . . . . . . 75
7. Our Wolf Ethic Inheritance
   Andrew Gulliford . . . . . . . . . . . . . . . . . . . . . 91
8. A New Mexico Homescape Land Ethic
   Richard Rubin. . . . . . . . . . . . . . . . . . . . . . . 101
9. Taos Community National Monument
   Richard Rubin. . . . . . . . . . . . . . . . . . . . . . . 117
10. Exploring Querencia as a Land Ethic
    Leeanna Torres . . . . . . . . . . . . . . . . . . . . . 129

Afterword by Richard Rubin . . . . . . . . . . . . . . 145
References. . . . . . . . . . . . . . . . . . . . . . . . . . . . 151
End Notes . . . . . . . . . . . . . . . . . . . . . . . . . . . 155

# Foreword
## Learning and Living Leopold's Legacy

Andrew Gulliford

In this personal book crafted to share the story of Aldo Leopold and his family with readers who may not know the Leopold legacy, while also weaving in his own experiences of living in northern New Mexico, Dr. Richard Rubin brings together diverse quotes, commentaries, and accomplishments of Leopold and *A Sand County Almanac*. I met Richard in Tres Piedras in front of the bungalow Leopold had built for his wife Estella in 1912. This book contains many references to the house and it is indeed the *querencia*, the refuge, that Leopold, then Supervisor of the Carson National Forest, intended the bungalow now known as Mi Casita to become.

Richard has performed an important voluntary service by helping maintain the house and grounds, leading tours, arranging repairs, and providing funding for the brass historic plaque that honors the bungalow and its designation on the National Register of Historic Places. He is an excellent steward of the house as well as a steward of Leopold's legacy having served on the board for the Albuquerque-based Leopold Writing Program. Environmental pilgrims from around the world have traveled to The Shack in Wisconsin where Leopold taught his family valuable conservation lessons and where he wrote most of *A Sand County Almanac,* but Aldo Leopold and his family also have deep connections in New Mexico and in this book, Richard explores many of those. Mi Casita in New Mexico is as important in Leopold's life as the Shack in Wisconsin. In this book you will learn about both.

While the Shack is now part of a much larger conservation area, Mi Casita was built at the base of the *Tres Piedras* or three famous granite rock outcroppings known to Native peoples, Spanish explorers, and trappers and traders moving across the vast sagebrush-covered plain to the northwest of the Rio Grande River. "There are two things that interest me: the relation of people to each other, and the relation of people to land," wrote Aldo Leopold in *A Sand County Almanac.* As one of the twentieth century's top conservationists and ecologists, Leopold's life and legacy continue to influence the environmental movement. His conservation thinking began to crystallize at Mi Casita along with a love story that almost ended in tragedy.

Educated at Yale, Aldo Leopold became one of the first

generation of young foresters. Leopold proved himself on the Apache National Forest in Arizona, and in 1911 he caught the eye of District Forester Arthur "Ring" Ringland who invited him to Albuquerque. The two handsome bachelors walked into a local drugstore only to be swept away by a pair of Hispanic sisters who were leaving the store. What they said to each other is lost to history, but Aldo was invited to a fancy dance or cotillion by Estella Luna Otero Bergere. He went.[1]

They danced and she stole his heart. "Ring" Ringland saw sparks between the couple and rather than assign Leopold to another Arizona forest, he assigned him as assistant supervisor of the 9,000 square mile Carson National Forest, which stretches from north of Santa Fe to the Colorado state line. Headquarters for the Carson were in Antonito, Colorado, and Leopold regularly rode the Denver & Rio Grande Railroad between Santa Fe and Antonito. He called it "slower'n a burro and just as sorry."

His job was to bring rules and regulations to abused and overgrazed forest lands where gullies "scissored across the landscape," but always in his thoughts was the young Estella. She had a second suitor, also Yale-educated. Leopold said of attorney H.B. "Jamie" Jamison that, "Jamie's soul is like a silk-covered brick." Their rivalry intensified and so did the need to stop overgrazing. On the Carson established in 1908, stockmen requested 220,000 sheep be permitted. The new plan allowed for only 198,000.

By 1900 the Upper Rio Grande may have been the most heavily grazed watershed in the country with 220,000 cattle and 1.7 million sheep, making it the heart of public land sheep grazing. "The families that for three and four generations had run the sheep outfits there were among the wealthiest in the West," wrote Leopold's biographer Curt Meine.[2] How ironic that Leopold, a young forester and conservationist, sought to marry into one of those families. Estella Luna Otero Bergere was heiress to one of the great sheep empires in the West. Her grandfathers Don Jose Luna and Don Jose Otero trailed 50,000 sheep to the Sierras after the California Gold Rush. Worth 50 cents apiece in New Mexico, they sold their flocks for $15 a head.[3]

Estella wouldn't answer his letters. Aldo took the train to Santa Fe and formally proposed. She attended Albuquerque's largest social event with her other suitor, but then that night, at 4:30 in the morning, she wrote Aldo and accepted. Marriage to Estella would be the most important event in Leopold's life.

Aldo Leopold achieved a stunning career in forestry, wildlife management, wilderness preservation, landscape restoration, and what we now call conservation biology and ecosystem management. But never again did he live in the bungalow he built against the pines. Instead, I have lived there as a writer who received an Aldo and Estella Leopold Writing Residency. Restored by the U.S. Forest Service in 2006, Leopold's house has wood floors, period leather furniture, a massive fireplace, a downstairs bedroom with plenty of light, extra beds upstairs, and a broad front porch where I ate every meal. The residency program is a collaboration with the Carson National Forest in fulfillment of the restoration mandate for Mi Casita to be a place of environmental inspiration and scholarship for Leopold's legacy. I was honored to be chosen for the fifth annual residency to work on my book manuscript on sheep and public lands grazing.[4]

With no telephone, cell service, internet, radio, or television, I felt like I'd entered a monastery. I'd write, walk my two dogs in a pine forest west of the house, write, eat lunch, write, and walk the dogs again. In the morning, sunlight bathed the house. By 3 P.M. when summer monsoons arrived, huge banks of dark blue-gray clouds washed over the horizon with curtains of rain or virga not quite touching the ground.

Leopold would recognize Tres Piedras now. It hasn't changed much. The D & RG's wooden water tower is still there, and you can get a good breakfast burrito at the Chili Line Depot Cafe. The road in front of the house is now U.S. highway 285, but aside from that ribbon of asphalt, most everything is as it was a century ago. San Antone Mountain to the north rises above a sea of sagebrush. Rio Grande del Norte National Monument to the east stretches across the Taos Plateau.[5]

I soaked up Leopold's essence in the historic house he built for his bride. A friend did a bird count finding twenty-nine birds near the bungalow including a Pygmy Nuthatch, Plumbeous Vireo, Hammond's Flycatcher, Townsend's Solitare, and a Western Wood-Pewee. At night I wrote in my journal and read *Stories from the Leopold Shack: Sand County Revisited* by Estella B. Leopold, the youngest of the five siblings.[6]

One evening with the windows open both dogs barked and growled quietly. Probably a bobcat passing through. The next morning, we hiked into the forest seeing the occasional can scatter from decades ago, finding an old wagon trace running west, pine cones stacked in a dry stock tank. Flickers flew between tall trees. I heard the raucous quork of ravens and the soft call of mourning doves, which like many other birds had been happily nibbling on seeds from the native plant garden Richard led the Taos Native Plant Society chapter to restore in front of Mi Casita.

When I applied for the residency, I was the same age Aldo Leopold was when he died. I wanted to finish what he started—an understanding of sheepherding, sheepmen, and their impacts on public landscapes. His time on the Carson National Forest deeply affected the future trajectory of Leopold's life and work. As a young, brash forester he came west to change the land, but instead the land changed him. He wrote that the oldest task in human civilization is to live on a piece of land without spoiling it. Now we have climate change. Migratory birds arrive and plants flower weeks earlier than expected.

Leopold's thoughts still guide us. His emphasis on the Land Ethic resonates across America with a new focus on eating local and organic farm-to-table products. For my final dinner in his house my wife cooked elk shoulder roast from a previous hunt. In the twilight we sat outside on the porch until stars came out above the Sangres; I wish Aldo Leopold could have been there.

Richard Rubin helps us to understand Leopold's Land Ethic legacy in New Mexico, but as he accurately states, Leopold's impact stretches across the nation and now the world. One more example of that legacy is the Endangered Species Act which Leopold did not live to see implemented, but which boldly reflects his ideas and his succinct statement in *A Sand County Almanac* that argues the first law of intelligent tinkering is to keep all the parts.

Fifty years ago, a bipartisan Congress did the right thing by a vote of 482 to 12. Congress passed, and President Richard Nixon signed, one of the most important pieces of environmental legislation in American history. The Endangered Species Act (ESA) of 1973 was a far-reaching law designed not only to protect animal and plant species that might be threatened or endangered, but also to reintroduce those species into their previous habitats. That legislation has had enormous ecological impacts and is one of the reasons gray wolves have been returned to Colorado.

The law is basically about humility and a national belief that our legacy as Americans includes the original plants, animals, and insects found in our fifty states. For a century after the Declaration of Independence in 1776 we ran roughshod over the continent erecting fences, killing bison and passenger pigeons, mining, logging, and building a nation. By the 1890s a conservation movement was born to make better use of our natural resources. How could we be more efficient? How could we waste less grass, timber, water and soil?

"We are not building this country of ours for a day. It is to last through the ages. We stand on the threshold of a new century," Theodore Roosevelt said in 1903. An ardent believer in conservation, TR saved 230 million acres of public land for all Americans, but even though he was an expert on birds and big mammals, he did not understand the predator-prey relationship. Roosevelt did not realize the role of predators in helping to maintain healthy populations of deer and elk. Native peoples understood that role, but not America's scientists. Not yet. It would be decades later in the 1950s and 1960s before the conservation movement evolved into the environmental movement and ecology became widely understood.

Finally, for the first time, we were concerned not just with protecting natural resources for our own use as Americans but in preserving the environment itself. In his book *A Sand County Almanac,* Aldo Leopold used the phrase "land ethic" and "land health," and he believed we should manage landscapes to contain the most species possible. His son Starker Leopold in The Leopold Report prepared for the National Park Service in 1963 argued that wildlife in national parks should be "a vignette of primitive America" and that all species belong.

A decade later, Congress passed the Endangered Species Act, which is "in some ways the most remarkable of our environmental laws," according to legal scholar John Leshy, Distinguished Professor Emeritus from the University of California. He adds,

> Strictly focused on saving what many consider God's creation—and perhaps for that reason enjoying deep and wide bipartisan support—its powerful commands operate only if an endangered species is formally "listed" by federal wildlife officials. As efforts to protect the sage grouse show, this can be a powerful incentive to undertake voluntary efforts to safeguard species, so as to avoid "listing."

## FOREWORD

In the United States, progressive change begins as an idea, becomes an ideal, and evolves into law. The Endangered Species Act represents a sweeping affirmation of ecological ethics, and it has had positive effects with the return of American eagles, bald eagles, peregrine falcons, alligators, Kirtland's warbler, and California condors.

Thanks to the law, I've heard the sharp calls of peregrines in Yampa Canyon and Echo Park in Dinosaur National Monument. I've seen condors returned to the Grand Canyon and to Marble Canyon where they fly both above and below historic Navajo Bridge. At Vermilion Cliffs National Monument in Arizona we camped for a week, walked the cliff rim, and saw so many condors it was hard to keep track of their wide wing spans as they rode thermal currents ever higher against the vast skies of the Colorado Plateau.

Yes, it is not easy living with endangered species. The tiny fish or snail darter stopped a few dams. There are rare flowers, rare rabbits, miniature owls, and even smaller bats, but small species can have big impacts. The diminutive cactus ferruginous pygmy owl sparked the Sonoran Desert Conservation Plan. Room to roam for endangered desert tortoises has halted motorcycle rallies and sprawling residential developments.

"People sometimes complain about how long a species remains listed under the ESA; we need to recognize how long it took to get a species to the point of being imperiled," comments Gary Skiba of the San Juan Citizens Alliance. With over thirty years of experience as a wildlife biologist, Skiba states, "The ESA is often cited as one of our most effective environmental laws, and it is. We need to keep it strong to help ensure that future generations can enjoy our wildlife heritage."

Since 1973 we have saved fifty-eight species, but we've also lost and are losing species to extinction. How tragic that in Theodore Roosevelt and Aldo Leopold's time the Bureau of Biological Survey ran a special laboratory in Denver to create predator poisons like strychnine. That same federal agency is now the U.S. Fish and Wildlife Service dedicated to species protection. Their professional staff make critical decisions during a ninety-day review as to whether a species should be listed as threatened or endangered. Across the West there have been fights over listing the Greater Sage Grouse. Now nationwide the once prevalent bumblebee is in trouble.

There have been successes with the ESA as well as losses, but conservationist and founder of the Sonoran Institute Luther Propst believes,

> The Endangered Species Act has served the United States and the world remarkably well for 50 years as the public policy "Emergency Room" for plants and animals. Without doubt, the ESA is one of the most important and effective statutory foundations for protecting wildlife, wildlife habitat, and life on Earth.

He adds, "We are all fortunate that leaders of both parties had the foresight to pass the act."

So where do we go from here? We keep the law intact. We leave the U.S. Fish & Wildlife Service in charge. As we struggle with climate change and global warming, let's try

FOREWORD

to save all the plants and animals we can for our twenty-first century Noah's ark, also known as spaceship Earth. Half a century ago, our politicians had extraordinary prescience, in part because of the philosophy and scientific studies of Aldo Leopold.

We need to continue to learn from Aldo Leopold and try to implement The Land Ethic. This delightful and meaningful book is an important effort in that direction. Leopold wrote that he needed "all things natural, wild and free." He did not live long enough for genetically modified foods or GMOs. In his era tractors were still small and hedgerows offered cover and habitat for wildlife. The so-called "Green Revolution" had not yet brought fence to fence farmin with tons of pesticides and fertilizers applied to over-used soils and the cutting down of windbreaks across the plains and prairies. Leopold had supervised some of the Civilian Conservation Corps who planted those trees and shrubs. His native state of Iowa where he grew up is now less than 7 percent natural habitat. Instead, it is all corn and soybeans. In the twenty-first century more than ever we need to understand and implement Leopold's Land Ethic. This modest *New Mexico Land Ethic Handbook* by Richard Rubin, with additions by Leeanna Torres and myself, contributes in important, personable ways.

———

Andrew Gulliford is a professor of history at Fort Lewis College in Durango, Colorado where he specializes in conservation and public land research and teaching. Reach him at gulliford_a@fortlewis.edu.

xxi

# Introduction

## Richard Rubin

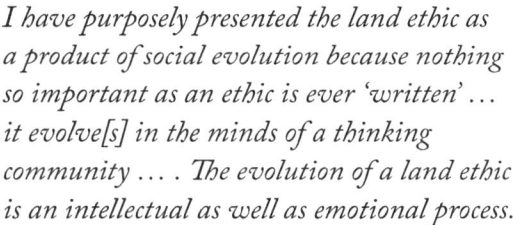

*I have purposely presented the land ethic as a product of social evolution because nothing so important as an ethic is ever 'written' … it evolve[s] in the minds of a thinking community … . The evolution of a land ethic is an intellectual as well as emotional process.*
— Aldo Leopold, *A Sand County Almanac* [1]

This Handbook is an odyssey through recent thoughts, experiences, and practices of the Land Ethic in Northern New Mexico. We view our subject as evolved since Aldo Leopold's early twentieth century time here. The term Land Ethic was coined by Leopold whose Forest Service career began briefly in Arizona and then progressed for thirteen years in New Mexico. This period from 1909 to 1924 has been described in biographies and extensive academic literature. However, these years were just the beginning of his now famous conservation practices, science, and ecological philosophy work. Aldo is best known for the 1949 classic *A Sand County Almanac,* plus hundreds of essays. The Aldo Leopold Foundation in Baraboo, Wisconsin, based on his "Shack" lands, continues public awareness of his legacy.[2]

While scholars have described how Leopold wrote explanations and justifications for the Land Ethic concept, his operational demonstrations were only beginning.

Applying Leopold's wisdom for personal human responsibility, this Handbook explores how examples of his Land Ethic can be appreciated now in Northern New Mexico. The authors range through origins, commentaries, historical restoration, adventures in places, and pragmatic efforts that manifest Land Ethic qualities. We call this a Handbook to inform and guide citizens, travelers, students, and seekers about the contributions of Land Ethics in contemporary New Mexico and how to be part of their evolution. Leopold formulated the idea of "ecological conscience." We emphasize this practice in our "thinking community." Yes, there are many environmental and social justice issues to confront, but also meaningful land ethic consciousness to recognize.

The inspiration for this Handbook comes from the current mission of the home and headquarters Leopold built in 1912 when appointed supervisor of the sprawling Carson National Forest. His new Santa Fe spouse Maria Alvira Estella Bergere playfully named the house Mia Casita, now known simply as Mi Casita (my little house). Aldo designed the Craftsman style bungalow to blend in the natural setting and make connection with the environment. The house and Forest Service support structures were designated a National Historic Site in 1993. Of most importance to this Land Ethic Handbook, the current official mission of Mi Casita was redefined in the 2005 U.S. Forest Service Restoration Plan: "to be a place of conservation education, reflection, and scholarly pursuits for the public."

# INTRODUCTION

Yet in our time now of debate, discontent, political conflict, and social justice controversy, achievements and contributions from a Land Ethic perspective seem clouded, even lost from public view. Not to indulge commercial boosterism or neglect genuine threats, we intend this Handbook to recognize hopeful Northern New Mexico Land Ethic stories. We hope these authentic views contribute to progress. Augmented by my career as a physician, I value Aldo's insight that our own health depends on the land's health. I also include several examples of brief opinion essays I have published recently in the Taos News, as examples of my practice sharing community enhancement thoughts inspired by Leopold's advocacy. Going beyond Leopold's articulate explanations and philosophy, the Handbook authors explore here authentic outcomes to Leopold's teachings. The contributors represent extensive experience and scholarship in New Mexico culture and history, as well as understanding of the Leopolds' influence here.

The chapters begin with a review of Leopold's classic "Land Ethic" essay in *A Sand County Almanac*. While Leopold used lower case in writing about the Land Ethic, as the title theme of this book, I elevate it to a proper noun.

Second, I take a diverse look at some modern scholars' thinking about ethics, applications to ecology, and commentary on Leopold's continuing relevance.

Next, I summarize how the Land Ethic is currently interpreted and implemented at the Leopold Foundation in Baraboo, Wisconsin. This is where he sought to study and restore depleted farmland, discovering observations for the *Almanac* and maturing his thinking.

Then we come home for a Northern New Mexico Land Ethic survey and *paseando,* meaning attentive walkabout. I begin with significant experiences in Aldo's early Arizona formative years in 1909, then New Mexico in 1911. I proceed through his Carson Forest appointment, marriage to Estella in Santa Fe, brief Mi Casita home time in Tres Piedras, near-fatal health challenge on range patrol, then Forest Service duties in Albuquerque. Our emphasis is recognition of the evolving Land Ethic values Leopold began to formulate here. I am pleased to share stories of Estella's cultural legacy recently provided by her daughter, also Estella.

One of his most significant Land Ethic initiatives began in the Albuquerque years, the philosophical and political achievement of the first official public land wilderness designation in the Gila National Forest in 1924. This northern survey includes our personal experiences in the Gila, Pecos, San Pedro Parks, Wheeler, and Columbine-Hondo areas close to home.

Professor Andrew Gulliford reviews the complex historic events and politics in the Gila Wilderness since establishment, as well as his own immersion as an outdoorsman. As Leopold prophesied, both the benefits and challenges of wilderness continue to reinforce our Almanac relevance.

In the next chapter, as evolved from Leopold's profound "green fire" insight, Andrew will trace the course of wolf extirpation in Colorado and the contemporary conflicts about restoration. The story in Colorado has been well documented for our education, but wolves range beyond stateline boundaries and are often observed now in northern New Mexico. Our ethical ecology consciousness continues necessary.

Beyond government and organization entities, individual people can pursue Land Ethics in their personal homescape practices. Leopold often asserted the responsibilities of private landowners. Homescape means the conjunction of the land we live on and our cultures expressed there. We will report some useful methods that the principal author applies for Leopold's categories of soil, water, plants, and animals.

In addition, despite the current controversies and conflicts around public lands, we recognize Land Ethic values in the preservation of national monuments. We honor our Taos County protected entity, the Rio Grande National Monument.

A summary chapter explores the Land Ethic qualities in the traditional Northern New Mexico devotion of *querencia*. Native Hispanic daughter Leeanna Torres expresses her experience and insights.

You may note in this list omission of Native American ethical relations to the land and sovereignty principles. The contributing authors do not feel adequate as spokespeople out of our own New Mexico cultural experience. Scholar Enrique Lamadrid provides these thoughts from Leopold's initially unpublished 1923 essay "Some Fundamentals of Conservation in the Southwest" relevant to New Mexico:

> "Five races-five cultures- have flourished here. We may truthfully say of our four predecessors that they left the earth alive, undamaged. Is it possibly a proper question for us to consider what the sixth shall say about us?'"

Ahead of his time, at the 1934 dedication of the University of Wisconsin Arboretum and Wildlife Sanctuary, one of his first duties as faculty, Leopold's biographer Curt Meine records:

> The most poignant moment in the ceremony came when Chief Albert Yellow Thunder, a native Ho-Chunk, appeared in full ceremonial regalia, and addressed the gathering. "My people are like the trees," he said, "a dying race, leaving behind them as their only monument the natural forests and streams of America." The natives, like the wolf, might not return to the land, but the arboretum could at least remind future generations that they were once there.[3]

Here are my thoughts on community with our landed cultures now, originally published in the *Taos News*, December 28, 2023. I intentionally have included in this book brief essays originally written following Aldo's model. He often used newsletters such as the Carson Forest *Pine Cone* and talks to organizations for sharing his evolving land ethic ideas.

### Honoring Many Human Truths

Admired and prolific Taos News columnist Cindy Brown in a November 30 *High Country Life* article wrote "Archaeologists say that ancestors of the Taos Pueblo people have been here for at least a thousand years. The current Pueblo structures were built between 1000 and 1450 c.e. The Pueblo people themselves say that they have been here

# INTRODUCTION

since time immemorial." The right and wrong of these alternate views have been argued and even turned into political land claims. Western archaeologists have been accused of representing European colonizers. Some people discount the Native views as primitive religion. I believe our world is enriched by honoring these as different types of truth. I claim no expertise, only offer some diverse thoughts.

Such differences are common in world cultures. Scientific scholars state the age of *Homo sapiens* is 200 to 300 thousand years. Evangelical Christians date the Earth and people at about six thousand years from the Biblical account. Orthodox Jews say we are in year 5784 since Creation. The *Preservation Archaeology Today* newsletter of December 20 describes how the Hopi migrations followed divine prophecy that led the ancestral clans to their current mesas a thousand years ago. Annette and I explored the beauty of Canyon de Chelly in 1968 when working on the Navajo Nation and learned their creation stories. The ancestral beliefs of the Mayans were fascinating to famous Taos author Frank Waters. There are many more powerful human culture legends.

Presence in Taos since *time immemorial* is frequently stated by Pueblo members and many others in our community as gestures of respect. My unabridged traditional dictionary defines immemorial as "extending back beyond memory, record, or knowledge." However, UNM archaeological publications describe the northern Tewa tribe's migration from the middle Rio Grande area for better water and hunting. Their settlement here a thousand years ago could be described as colonizing common lands used by other tribes, seasonal nomads following cycles of food and climate. Many remnants of their pit and jacal houses have been identified in Taos Valley.

Hmm, those words settler and colonizer have become derogatory in today's politics. But the alternative description and justification as indigenous is an area of complex debate among scholars. Who qualifies in a particular place, and after how long? Maybe the actions of settlers and colonizers rather than category names should influence our judgments, such as peaceful or exploitive. Maybe the judgments with these terms change over time. I grew up in New Jersey and attended a high school founded in 1774 to educate future leaders for the new colony's independence from the British Empire. Continuing into my much later tenure, our mascot was a Minuteman carrying books and a musket. Yes, the settler colonists had taken the Native tribes' land, but I think our democracy's rebellion from monarchy had merit. Social philosophers might call this "value pluralism," meaning both are correct but in conflict with each other.

# INTRODUCTION

> So as we enter a new year with serious threats and struggles in the world, I advocate honoring the multiple types of truth, wisdom, and belief that can coexist. As thirteenth century Persian Islamic poet Rumi said, "Beyond right and wrong, there is a field. I'll meet you there."

This Handbook's principal author, Richard Rubin, is grateful to have received Mi Casita inspiration through personal experience. I've been the steward there for seven years as an authorized U.S. Forest Service volunteer. Maintenance projects began with simple native plant restoration, painting, and rodent control for visiting writer residents. At Tres Piedras U.S. Forest Service ranger invitation, I organized a volunteer services group called the Friends of Mi Casita and established a dedicated fund at the Taos Community Foundation.[4] This has provided resources for interior safety carpentry, warped porch floor replacement, chimney liner installation to meet code, a new stove, rodent proofing, and improved access keypad locks. The annual linseed oiling of the porch rails is a meaningful activity. It is inspiring to work in sight of the Sangre de Cristos to the east.

As steward, I also provide tours for student groups and community organizations. Besides adding to their education, my guidance is necessary due to the U.S. Forest Service restriction on Mi Casita access. Making rounds on the property weekly year-round provides me immersion with the land and its more-than-human occupants. In addition, a small library of books by and about Leopold was donated to the Tres Piedras District U.S. Forest Service by the Albuquerque Wildlife Federation in 2012.[5] This contribution provided inspiration for me to foster the library's growth as Writing Program residents, my own scholarship additions, and various donors provided many more books, fulfilling the Mi Casita mission of education and conservation inspiration.

The U.S. Forest Service has committed to greater Mi Casita public access. The ranger station lobby and small gazebo at the house show informative displays. Funding has

been obtained through the Infrastructure Act for fire-retardant roof shingle and old septic tank replacement in 2024. Overnight stays through the U.S. Forest Service national rental program will be announced eventually. Influenced by my career as a physician, I feel devoted to the health of Mi Casita and her legacy.

I express much gratitude to this small book's contributors. In addition to their extensive scholarship, literary skills, and teaching accomplishments, Leeanna Torres and Professor Andrew Gulliford have immersed themselves as Leopold Writing Program residents at Mi Casita. I also acknowledge the permission by the *Taos News* for reprinting essays in this community nonprofit book and the Wisconsin based Aldo Leopold Foundation for their endorsement of our Sand County Almanac 75th anniversary recognition.

Dr. Richard Rubin
Arroyo Seco, New Mexico, 2024

# The Land Ethic
## in Leopold's Words

Richard Rubin

The principal expression of the Land Ethic appeared in the essays appended to *A Sand County Almanac*. Recognizing several editions, I use here the paperback publication (2020) by Oxford University Press titled *A Sand County Almanac and Sketches Here and There*. It features an Introduction by Barbara Kingsolver, and I quote her closing lines:

> He may help you see past the frustrating divides that plague the awfullest failure of our day, as we try to reconcile human subsistence with the needs of our damaged biological home. If you've lost all hope of finding a common language for that conversation, you might well find it here.[6]

This edition is likely the one most actively sold now through commercial sources, including the Aldo Leopold Foundation store. The Almanac monthly essays are listed as Part I, Sketches Here and There are Part II, and Part III is titled The Upshot. The Land Ethic is the final essay;

components are The Ethical Sequence, The Community Concept, The Ecological Conscience, Substitutes for a Land Ethic, The Land Pyramid, Land Health and the A-B Cleavage, and The Outlook. It comprises twenty-two pages in this paperback edition.

I select here passages most meaningful to my experience of the Land Ethic in New Mexico. I follow the essay chronology as published. The quotations are chosen to enhance our process of understanding Land Ethics. Our goal is capturing the emotional as well as intellectual. Much of the material omitted is his examples and illustrations.

Leopold introduces the idea of ethical ecology evolution.

## The Ethical Sequence

> This extension of ethics, so far studied only by philosophers, is actually a process in ecological evolution. (pp. 190–191).

For perspective, I note a traditional dictionary definition of ethics from my Unabridged 1966 *Random House Dictionary*.

> Ethic, *singular noun:* 1) the body of moral principles or values governing or distinctive of a particular culture or group; 2) a complex of moral precepts held or rules of conduct followed by an individual.

And under Ethics *plural noun*, I find closer to Leopold:

> 4) that branch of philosophy dealing with values relating to human conduct, with respect to the rightness and wrongness of certain actions and to the goodness and badness of the motives and ends of such actions.

## The Community Concept

> The land ethic simply enlarges the boundaries of the community to include soils, waters, plants, and animals, or collectively: the land … . In short, a land ethic changes the role of *Homo sapiens* from conqueror of the land-community to plain member and citizen of it. (p. 192).

These statements are among the most often quoted. Since written in the 1940s, our contemporary gender and social justice concerns require some clarification. Masculine terms were the convention of the time. Commentators have challenged implications of the word "citizen" as reflecting social injustice hierarchies. I do not believe Leopold had a political or racist motive for distinguishing "citizens," but merely using a comprehensive word for people in the community. A writer friend recently quoted in the *Taos News* a Merriam Webster definition I like. Citizenship is "the quality of an individual's responsibility or contribution to his community." However, as Kimberly Ruffin who was a Leopold Writing Program resident at Mi Casita asserts in *Black on Earth: African American Ecoliterary Traditions*,[7] we need to inform our thinking with awareness of human and non-human ecological injustices to be truly ethical.

Leopold continues:

## The Ecological Conscience

> Conservation is a state of harmony between men and land. … . Obligations have no meaning without conscience, and the problem we face is the extension of the social conscience from people to land (p. 196).

## Substitutes for a Land Ethic

> One basic weakness in a conservation system based wholly on economic motives is that most members of the land community have no economic value. Wildflowers and songbirds are examples … . Yet these creatures are members of the biotic community, and if (as I believe) its stability depends on its integrity, they are entitled to continuance … . (p. 198).

> There is a clear tendency in American conservation to relegate to government all necessary jobs that private landowners fail to perform … . The answer, if there is any, seems to be in a land ethic, or some other force which assigns more obligation to the private landowner (pp. 200–201).

Following this assertion, we include in a later chapter personal practices on our homescape.

## The Land Pyramid

> We can be ethical only in relation to something we can see, feel, understand, love, or otherwise have faith in (p. 202).

> Land, then, is not merely soil; it is a fountain of energy flowing through a circuit of soils, plants, and animals (p. 203).

## Land Health and the A-B Cleavage

> A land ethic, then, reflects the existence of an ecological conscience, and this in turn reflects a conviction of individual responsibility for the health of the land. (p. 208).

This powerful view is an extraordinary ideal. That being said, recent disability rights advocates have criticized the insufficient regard for impaired health as a fixed condition, not possible to renew, and therefore discriminatory. As a physician and handicapped child parent, I see a spectrum of capacity for renewal, diverse adaptation, and creative individuality. Yes, some of our land may be permanently disabled, yet evolution is an ongoing process. Continuing:

> In all these cleavages, we see repeated the same basic paradoxes: man the conqueror *versus* man the biotic citizen; science the sharpener of his sword *versus* science the searchlight on his universe; land the slave and servant *versus* land the collective organism (Leopold's italics, p. 210).

## The Outlook

> It is inconceivable to me that an ethical relation to land can exist without love, respect, and admiration for land, and a high regard for its value. By value, I of course mean something far broader than mere economic value; I mean value in the philosophical sense (p. 210).

And another of the most quoted statements:

> *A thing is right when it tends to preserve the integrity, stability, and beauty of the biotic community. It is wrong when it tends otherwise* (author's italics, p. 211).

Ending our selections from the essay:

> I have purposely presented the land ethic as a product of social evolution because nothing so important as an ethic is ever "written." … . tentative because evolution never stops (p. 212).

The authors present this Handbook for continuing evolution of Land Ethic intellectual and emotional process, tangible manifestations, and useful achievements.

# Selected Land Ethic Commentary
## Richard Rubin

### The Biblical Controversy

Leopold thought deeply about human impact on the environment. His assertion of Biblical influence enabling land exploitation has provoked divergent views. At an extreme, the Deep Ecology movement attributes our Anthropocene to the Biblical dominion axiom quoted below. I have been wrestling with this issue since discovering Aldo's statement in the 1948 Foreword to *A Sand County Almanac:*[8]

> We abuse land because we regard it as a commodity belonging to us. When we see land as a community to which we belong, we may begin to use it with love and respect (p. xxii).

These commodity and community epithets have become common vocabulary among environmental thinkers and advocates. The previous sentence in the Foreword, rarely quoted, is the one most troubling to my consciousness:

> Conservation is getting nowhere because it is incompatible with our Abrahamic concept of land (p. xxii).

Even more overlooked in this conversation is the original passage from Leopold's 1947 manuscript Foreword, later abbreviated due to publisher rejections. I quote Aldo's words as published by J. Baird Callicott, editor, *Companion to A Sand County Almanac:*[9]

> Art and letters, ethics and religions, law and folklore still regard the wild things of the land either as enemies, or as food, or as dolls to be kept for pretty. This view of land is our inheritance from Abraham, whose foothold in the land of milk and honey was still a precarious one, but it is outmoded for us. Our foothold is precarious, not because it may slip, but because we may kill the land before we learn to use it with love and respect (Appendix p. 282).

The relevant text in the King James Bible, Genesis verse 1:26, states:

> So God created man in his image, male and female he created them. And God blessed them, and God said unto them, Be fruitful and multiply, and replenish the earth and subdue it: and have dominion over the fish of the sea and over the fowl of the air, and over every living thing that moveth upon the earth.

However, another statement in *The Ethical Sequence* section of the Land Ethic essay shows Leopold's broader Bible interest than this Abrahamic dominion text. Historically, the later prophets he quotes lived a millennium after the Abrahamic Genesis events were said to occur.

> Individual thinkers since the days of Ezekiel and Isaiah have asserted that the despoliation of land is not only inexpedient but wrong. Society, however, has not yet affirmed their belief. I regard the present conservation movement as the embryo of such an affirmation.[10]

Biographer Curt Meine describes a significant phase of Leopold's Bible scholarship.

> He had a particular fondness for the Old Testament prophets, proverbs, and psalms. Ever on the lookout for historical evidence, he also found the Old Testament an abundant source of information on natural history. In April 1920, as the forest inspection season began, the *Journal of Forestry* published an article by Leopold entitled "The Forestry of the Prophets." Leopold's article was more than just a playful combination of Bible study and natural history. The Bible, like the explorers' journals he was also reading at this time, rendered real lessons about the relationship between man and his environment over time (op. cit., p. 183).

I interpret Leopold's warning about the Biblical dominion command as persuasion for us to exercise moral choice in our relationship with the land, not indulge exploitive entitlement. This is the essence of an ethic.

## Wholistic versus Individual Species Rights

British philosophy and literature professor Peter Marshall in *Nature's Web: Rethinking Our Place on Earth*[11] congratulates Leopold for providing a scientific basis to an environmental ethic. He observes that Leopold extended the right to life to the whole biotic community. However, in Leopold's calling for restraint and care in human dealings with the environment, Marshall identifies risks. He quotes Leopold scholar J. Baird Callicott:

> The land ethic is important because it is holistic and has as its objective "the good of the community of the whole." Such ethical holism calculates right and wrong in relation not to individuals but to the biotic community (p. 356).

Marshall summarizes:

> What is urgently required is an environmental ethic which is holistic in orientation, but which is not ready to sacrifice individuals to the wellbeing of the whole; an ethic which gives equal consideration to the interests of humans and nonhumans without losing sight of the collective interests of the wider community in which they live. Such an ethic should be based on the principle of reverence for all life. While trying to minimize suffering, it would attempt to maximize the wellbeing of the ecosphere and help realize the evolutionary potential of nature as a whole (p. 357).

Marshall also observes limitations to Leopold's "originality," debts to Darwin and Schweitzer, and inadequate attention to the "clash" between the right to life and the right to property. Yet he concludes:

> But Leopold's enormous influence is probably due to the fact that he was a woodsman who spoke poetically to the general public, evoking a deep love of nature. He was prepared to query the ethical roots of existing conservation practices. He extended the so-called natural rights enjoyed by all Americans to the rights of nature itself. He challenged the great frontier tradition of America, calling for restraint and care in dealings with the environment. Above all, he rejected the conqueror role of man in the Judeo-Christian tradition and argued that "men are fellow-voyagers with other creatures in the odyssey of evolution" (p. 355).

Aldo's full expression of this idea occurs in the *A Sand County Almanac* essay "Wisconsin," under subtitle "On a Monument to the Pigeon:"

> It is a century now since Darwin gave us the first glimpse of the origin of species. We know now what was unknown to all the preceding caravan of generations: that men are only fellow-voyagers with other creatures in the odyssey of evolution. This new knowledge should have given us, by this time, a sense of kinship with fellow-creatures; a wish to live and let live; a sense of wonder over the magnitude and duration of the biotic enterprise. (p 102)

## From Land to Road Ethic

Environmental journalist Ben Goldfarb knows his Leopold. He has a masters degree from the Yale School of Environmental Science, the modern form of the Forestry School degree obtained by Aldo in 1908. Ben also spent a month at Mi Casita as a Leopold Writing Program resident.[12] In his new book *Crossings: How Road Ecology is Shaping the Future of Our Planet*,[13] Ben states that Leopoldian wilderness area protection from intrusive roads is a moral value:

> Roads, I began to realize, were not merely a symptom of civilization but a distinct disease. (p.7) ... . Road ecology is a call to deconstruct the derelict logging tracks that lace our forests (p. 12).
>
> Motorized transportation inflicts suffering on an almost unimaginable scale; there may be nothing humans do that causes more misery to more wild animals than driving ... . The practice of road ecology is not merely a set of engineering principles but a moral mandate (p. 215).

Ben then applies this insight to Leopold's mandate, his italics:

> "A thing is right," Aldo Leopold famously wrote in his call for a land ethic, "when it tends to preserve the integrity, stability, and beauty of the biotic community." By that standard, roads are the wrongest things imaginable, agents of chaos that shatter biotic integrity wherever they intrude. Perhaps we need an analogous *road* ethic, an

aphorism that pithily encapsulates what makes a road right and what makes it wrong. *A road is right when its planners have done everything within their power to avoid disrupting the biotic and human communities through which it passes, perhaps. Or A road is right when it, like its masters, belongs to the land instead of conquering it* (p. 296).

## Environmental Virtue Ethics

Scholars Ronald Sandler and Philip Cafaro edited *Environmental Virtue Ethics*.[14] In their introduction, environmental ethics are defined:

> … as a field of inquiry attempting to understand the human relationship with the environment (including natural ecosystems, agricultural ecosystems, urban ecosystems, and the individuals that populate and constitute those systems) and determine the norms that should govern our interactions with it. These norms can be either of action or character. The project of specifying the latter is *environmental virtue ethics,* and a particular account of the character dispositions that we ought to have regarding the environment is an *environmental virtue ethic* (p. 1–2).

> Environmental virtue is not merely valuable as the disposition to identify and then perform proper actions; it is also valuable in itself. It is life-affirming and life-enhancing (p. 3).

Rachel Carson is quoted:

> Those who dwell, as scientists or laymen, among the beauties and mysteries of the earth are never alone or weary of life (p.3).

Contributor Bill Shaw:

> … examines Leopold's land ethic—that one ought to promote the integrity, beauty and stability of the biotic community—from a virtue ethics perspective … . He suggests three land virtues—respect (or ecological sensitivity), prudence, and practical judgment (p. 9).

Phillip Cafaro states:

> Aldo Leopold can be interpreted as an environmental virtue ethicist … . While Leopold's classic essay "The Land Ethic" makes a moving plea for human self-restraint, he devotes much of *A Sand County Almanac* to showing the opportunities for knowledge and self-development made possible by a greater attentiveness to nature (p. 33).

Echoing the beginning of "The Land Ethic" essay, Shaw observes:

> In a way that parallels the admission of "slave girls" into the human fold, Leopold sees the protective cloak of the land ethic drawn warmly about the borders of neighboring communities. Communities that were once mere instruments, mere resources, mere property, are valued in a different light (p. 102).

## The Once and Future Land Ethic

Scholars and thought leaders have continued following Leopold's call that the Land Ethic should evolve in the minds of a thinking community. In the 2003 compendium *From Conquest to Conservation: Our Public Lands Legacy*,[15] Curt Meine and Nina Leopold Bradley provide an essay "The Once and Future Land Ethic." I quote these selected questions they pose:

> How must the land ethic evolve in order to thrive and guide conservation in the new century? … How do we encourage the land ethic within constantly changing human communities with diverse traditions and varied relationships to land? … How can we ensure that the land ethic will continue to absorb, reflect, and adapt to the insights that flow from the natural sciences? … How can we revive and strengthen bonds of common interest within the landscape and within conservation? … How can we extend the land ethic to embrace and encourage an "ocean ethic"? … How can the land ethic help to address the issue of population growth responsibly, respectfully, and effectively? … Can the land ethic have deep and meaningful impact on the human economic enterprise? … How will changes in education and in society affect the next generation's sense of personal engagement? How can we evoke a sense of local responsibility for the full spectrum of land values while stimulating cooperative measures to restore

and sustain land health? ... Finally, a thriving land ethic will draw on expressions of stewardship from diverse cultural sources (p. 119–120).

### **Land Ethic as Wholeness**

Our last commentary is from farmer, poet, philosopher Wendell Berry in his recent book *The Need To Be Whole:*[16]

> My thoughts at first were guided by my inherited inclination to see the good care of the land as the highest human obligation, and the good care of the human community as the second highest. These principles of mine were radically amplified, clarified, and set in order by my reading, many years ago, of Aldo Leopold's essay "The Land Ethic." That ethic, to one coming upon it in the midst of our darkened and disordered age, declares itself with the sudden brightness of obvious truth ... . And so we can say that, to make whole sense of any dispute between two merely human sides, the land-community must be represented, not as an equal third side, but as the side whose fate ultimately will decide the fate of the other sides (p. 9).

Now as we consider these meaningful words, let us journey to Land Ethic development and evolution of practices.

# Land Ethic
## Origin and Evolution
### Richard Rubin

**Arizona Territory**

Upon graduating from the Yale School of Forestry, Leopold was sent west to new national forests in 1909 when Arizona and New Mexico were still territories. Biographer Curt Meine records an event occurring in October of lasting import in Leopold's life. Andy Gulliford analyzes the contemporary importance of this further in Chapter 7 later in this book.

Briefly, leading a crew in the rugged Blue Range of the Apache Forest for several days of lumber inspection, Leopold shot a mother wolf and

> ... saw in the eyes of the wolf what he would describe years later as "a fierce green fire." The men moved closer. Leopold held out his rifle between himself and the dying wolf. In a final, instinctive upwelling of defiance, the wolf gnashed out and

> grabbed the rifle butt in its teeth. The men backed off. As they watched from a distance, the green fire died, but not before it had burned the moment into Leopold's psyche (Meine, p. 94).

Scholars and commentators have devoted much attention to this experience. The powerful essay Leopold wrote later in April 1944 was "Thinking Like a Mountain." An excellent portrayal can be seen in the 2011 DVD "Fierce Green Fire" available commercially. To appreciate the evolution of Leopold's views and relevance to our Land Ethic theme, readers can find the essay in the *A Sand County Almanac Part II, Sketches Here and There.*

## To New Mexico

When Leopold was appointed deputy supervisor of the 950,000-acre Carson National Forest in April of 1911, the upper Rio Grande was suffering from extremely heavy grazing, struggling forest regeneration, and soil erosion gullying the range. His chief challenge was implementing new grazing policies, authorized by a recent Supreme Court ruling that supported Federal regulation on the public forests. But first, Aldo courted and married Maria Alvira Estella Bergere from a politically prominent Santa Fe family, descended from generations of Lunas. The name *de Luna* was conferred by the Spanish king on a young capitano in 1091 when he defeated a Moorish fleet in a surprise attack by the light of the moon. Later, Don Tristan de Luna y Arellano of Castile sailed with Cortez to New Spain in 1530. He eventually became the governor of Spain's Florida colony. Then after the 1693 New Mexico Reconquista from the Pueblo Revolt of 1680, a branch of the Lunas acquired claim to eighty thousand acres of the San Clemente Land Grant in the Rio Abajo south of present-day Albuquerque. (Meine, p.111).

Aldo and Estella's youngest daughter, Estella B. Leopold, relates in her recent memoir *Aldo's Wife: Estella Bergere My Remarkable Mother*[17] that, in 1716, her great-grandfather Diego Luna bought the entire San Clemente Land Grant, around a million acres. Then she tells us:

> Around 1850, [ranch heir] Antonio Jose Luna and his cousin Antonio Jose Otero attempted a novel and bold experiment. They hired many sheepherders and sheepdogs, rounded up their combined flocks of about 50,000 sheep, and drove them westward over the desert and plains to California, where they sold the sheep at a good profit to people in the gold mining business….Immediately the Luna and Otero families became the *Ricos* (wealthy) people of the Rio Abajo [their hacienda became the town Los Lunas] (p. 9–10).

> Antonio Jose Luna married Isabella Baca of Belen after he returned from California in about 1852. Antonio and Isabella had several accomplished children. Two elder sons, Tranquilino and Solomon Luna, became active in politics and were heavily engaged in helping the New Mexico Territory obtain statehood (p. 10).

> Antonio and Isabella's youngest daughter Eloisa Luna (born 1864) was a favorite and an especially lovely young woman who later became Estella's mother (p. 11).

Estella B. Leopold provides insight into the intellectual backgrounds and life skills of her grandmother Eloisa and mother Estella that would later contribute to Aldo's achievements. In the late 1870s, Eloisa completed her high school education at a Catholic academy and then finishing school in New York City. Estella thrived at the Los Lunas hacienda among her siblings and cousins, an Irish governess, learning good horsemanship and the workings of the ranch. She attended St. Vincent's Academy in Albuquerque, and then a well-known Catholic high school in Cincinnati with her sister. This was followed by Maryville College in St. Louis.

Of cultural significance, her multilingual father Alfred Bergere was an accomplished pianist and taught Estella to play, praising her skill:

> Alfred would gather the children around the piano each afternoon, and he would lead them in song. Many of the songs were Mexican popular folk songs; examples were *Adelita, En Las Playas del Mar, Cuatro Milpas, Amorcito, Atotonilco, Donde estas Corazon?* And many others. There were many songs in praise of the Hispanic culture and about love, beautiful mountains, and happiness (p.28).

In addition, I learn:

> The Bergere family took occasional outings southward [from Santa Fe] to the Pecos Mountains to enjoy the forest and the Pecos River, a fine place to fish and camp (p. 28).

## Mi Casita Vision

Our Land Ethic journey follows Aldo in 1911 to the home that Estella playfully named "Mia Casita." It is now known simply as Mi Casita, "my little house." He developed plans for a Craftsman style bungalow aesthetic which employed features in contrast to decorative Victorian architecture, such as harmony with the setting, natural finish woods, and multiple windows open to the environment. Leopold situated the house against the middle of the three prominent rocks. The front porch view looks east across Taos Valley about thirty miles to the dramatic Sangre de Cristo Mountains. This planning of the site was *de novo* when Leopold moved the Carson headquarters to Tres Piedras from Antonito, Colorado.

So let's proceed on our vicarious *paseando*. While on the front porch, look north about 15 miles to a low rounded dome. Meine quotes a letter Aldo wrote to Estella during their 1911 courtship:

> San Antone Mountain was a great glory of bronze and gold- and the Taos Mountains—sixty continuous miles of main range under the eastern sky—ablaze with great masses of orange and crimson. I can hardly tell you what a blessed peace I find in my Sundays in the hills—I wouldn't be able to get along without them—something would break, I know (p. 116).

San Antonio Mountain is a free-standing volcanic peak of 10,908 feet in the Carson National Forest. Just west of it along the Rio San Antonio, 600-acre Stewart Meadows is managed by the NM Dept of Game and Fish as a wildlife refuge that includes deer, elk, and pronghorns. This former settlers' ranch was purchased in 1973 by the Carson National Forest. The Rio San Antonio has been recognized as an impaired stream; riparian vegetation improvements reduce water temperatures and stabilize bank erosion, as well as hopefully attract beavers.

Continuing our hike back around Mi Casita, observe many more than three old granite rocks. The Tres Piedras name derives from those standing out as landmarks seen from a distance, likely for millenia. The tallest named Mosaic is popular with rock climbers. Before European settlement, the Tewa name was "mountain sheep rock place." Closer to the house, many sheltered alcoves surely protected indigenous hunters, travelers, and wildlife. A Jicarilla Apache band apparently lived just south for a generation in the 1800s after Comanches and the U.S. Cavalry pushed them from the Cimarron area in the eastern mountains towards their eventual reservation lands in northwest

## LAND ETHIC ORIGIN AND EVOLUTION

New Mexico. Forest Service archaeologists have collected artifacts which are displayed in the nearby Ranger Station. However, no traditional population has settled here continuously due to the lack of reliable water before late nineteenth century ranching and logging interests began.

I have been curious about the origin of the Mosaic Rock name. Mi Casita is nestled against the middle of the three Tres Piedras rocks. Mosaic on the west dominates the view from all directions. It is approximately a half mile west, approached on Forest Road 64J which turns north just past the Ranger Station on Highway 64. My historical sources do not explain the name. I doubt the Hispanic explorers would have associated it with a Hebrew prophet rather than a Catholic saint. Some Googling identifies Mosaic Canyon in Death Valley National Park, named from the diverse geology formations due to a variety of mineral deposits. However, my amateur inspection of our rock shows uniform reddish-brown granite, not mixed.

My 1966 Unabridged Dictionary reveals, as a noun, *mosaic* definition #5 is "in architecture, a system of patterns used to separate areas according to function." Hmm, while reading the Fairfax edited text *Buying Nature: The Limits of Land Acquisition as a Conservation Strategy, 1790–2004*,[18] I find:

> In this book we will talk about mosaics of conserved land: combinations of different agents, targets, and tools of acquisition. Partnerships of public and private actors are revealed early on as a constant element of land conservation. Mosaics are a sign of further complexity—different types

> of land purchased by different acquirers, under varying terms and conditions, and managed to meet very different goals ... . The first mosaics of public and private land, called checkerboards, occurred where both the government and the grantees held onto their parcels (p. 5–6).

I am hearing echoes of Leopold and his interest in peoples' relationship to their land. I am sure he confronted local conflicts between early Forest Service retention of federal public domain ownership versus private property rights. This continues today. West central New Mexico has extensive checkerboard lands that are in contention between Navajo landowners, uranium mining interests, and protectors of the historic Chaco Canyon site.

Looking at a current Carson National Forest Tres Piedras District map, I see a private inholding of about one quarter square mile at the location of Mosaic Rock. There are many others as we look west and north on the map, not neatly surveyed checkerboard parcels, but definitely a mosaic. On the ground, primitive road 64J ends at a fence labeled private property. Hikers and rock climbers are allowed to proceed on the trail following posted rules, such as not disturbing nesting peregrine falcons. Uncertain of current ownership, locals tell me an old man lived in a shack there years ago.

I do not know if legendary Taos arts matron Mabel Dodge Lujan knew of Leopold's publications in New Mexico when she invited famous British writer D.H. Lawrence and his wife Frieda to New Mexico in 1922. As inducement to stay, she gave them a 160-acre property known as Kiowa Ranch in the mountains near the village of San Cristobal north of

Taos on the east side of the Rio Grande Gorge. They were here intermittently until 1925, and this D.H. Lawrence Ranch is now a national historic site owned by the University of New Mexico. Lawrence subsequently became known as a naturalistic craftsman of superb literary skill.

This may be the reason I found a small book on the shelf at Mi Casita that would have been left there sometime between the 2007 restoration and 2012, but with no inscription. It is *The Spirit of Place: An Anthology made by Richard Aldington from the Prose of D. H. Lawrence*, London, 1944. Lawrence wrote a novella *St. Mawr* at the Ranch in 1924, published in 1925.[19] The book's heroine left postwar dysphoric England and settled in the mountains near Taos. I share Lawrence's description of the view from 8600 feet at the Ranch across the Taos Valley looking towards Tres Piedras. This serendipitous literary discovery at Mi Casita complements Leopold's 1911 description to Estella during their courtship:

> Sometimes she would see the far-off rocks, thirty miles away, where the canyon made a gateway between the mountains. Quite clear, like an open gateway out of a vast yard, she would see the cut-out bit of the canyon passage. And on the desert itself, curious puckered folds of mesa-sides. And a blackish crack which in places revealed the otherwise invisible canyon of the Rio Grande. And beyond everything, the mountains like icebergs showing up from an outer sea. Then later, the sun would go down blazing above the shallow cauldron of simmering darkness, and the

> round mountain of Colorado would lump up into uncanny significance, northwards (p. 173).

## Crisis, Recovery, and Albuquerque Transition

From October 1912 to April 1913, the Leopolds were happy at Mi Casita. Estella learned new practical skills with "a somewhat shy but quite sizable sense of humor" as Aldo wrote to his father (Meine, p.122). Over winter, Aldo managed the new grazing permit applications and enjoyed the beautiful views, his great fireplace,[20] books, pipe, and the news Estella was carrying their first child. I imagine he found the setting's ecotone fascinating, observing the transition among ecological communities. But with spring, his field responsibilities included settling conflicts between the sheepherder permittees and Forest Service. On horseback in the Jicarilla District, he endured several days of snow and hailstorms. Becoming lost crossing the Apache Reservation attempting to meet the train at Chama, he endured severe leg swelling. Miraculously making the trip back to Tres Piedras on April 23, and barely alive, he was diagnosed at the hospital in Santa Fe with acute nephritis, Bright's Disease of the kidney. Pregnant Estella was with her family in Santa Fe then.

Aldo's recovery required sixteen months, primarily back at his family home in Burlington, Iowa with a Christmas interlude in Santa Fe. His scholarship and writing continued actively. We can glean Land Ethic progress in his ideas on conservation and the duties of the Forest Service from an article he wrote in the July 1913, Carson National Forest newsletter *Pine Cone:*

> We are entrusted with the protection and development, through wise use and constructive study, of the timber, water, forage, farm, recreative, game, fish, and aesthetic resources of the areas under our jurisdiction (Meine, p. 126).

On September 14, 1914, Leopold was reinstated by the Forest Service. Based in Albuquerque, he had responsibilities in the Office of Grazing and in charge of new fish and game policies. To abbreviate the long story, our Land Ethic odyssey can begin to appreciate Leopold's early work then for wildlife conservation. He did extensive travels throughout New Mexico organizing game protective associations and often contributing articles to the *Pine Cone* newsletter. As the Leopold family grew, they built a larger house at 135 Fourteenth St. SW, which had room for a garden and access to the Rio Grande. The neighborhood is now a state certified Aldo Leopold Historic Site.

**Towards Wildness**

Aldo's transition from game conservation to wildlife preservation began then. In a 1917 speech to the Albuquerque Rotary Club, he told the businessmen:

> "The ideal was to restore to every citizen his inalienable right to know and love the wild things of his native land" (Meine, p. 161).

As World War I changed the Forest Service, Aldo accepted the position of secretary to the Albuquerque Chamber of Commerce. Active with several civic organizations, he pursued speaking and writing about preservation of the city's distinctive culture and natural setting. One concern he had was the proposed draining of Rio Grande wetlands for expanded agriculture. We can credit this experience with his early advocacy against destruction of wild habitat. By 1918, his writings were the first published attempts to chart a future course for the conservation of wildlife in America, and to explain his view of the role of wildlife in modern society.

**Wilderness Beginnings**

By 1919, Leopold had been promoted to Forest Service District 3 Chief of Operations. His main task was inspection of individual forests and making management recommendations. We can use our historic imaginations to appreciate his brief visit that summer to the Carson Forest Taos District. That autumn, he also toured the Datil Forest which was established in 1908. This opportunity brought him into the headwaters of the Gila River. In December, Aldo had extensive discussions in Colorado with Arthur Carhart, a young Forest Service landscape architect who was initiating interest in forest preservation, rather than development.

Andrew Gulliford tells us more in Chapter 6, reporting about a 1919 meeting with Leopold. Carhart voiced his opinion that Trappers Lake in northwest Colorado should be left pristine and void of tourist cabins. Leopold liked the idea and eventually succeeded in establishing the Gila Wilderness in 1924. Thus began the evolution of American wilderness, "where man is a visitor who does not remain." Today, the Gila Wilderness encompasses 760,000 acres or 1,187 square miles. The western half retains the original name "Gila Wilderness." The Eastern portion was named the "Aldo Leopold Wilderness" in 1980.

## Erosion and Land Health

From Leopold's early days to his regional operations inspection duties, he often observed the rugged arroyos, gulleys, gulches, and ravines. His professional concern about serious erosion problems increased. While reducing overgrazing and cattle riparian intrusion were acknowledged Forest Service objectives, Leopold began to advocate efforts at range control and land restoration. From trips to the Apache and Sitgreaves National Forests in Arizona, the Tajique District of the Manzano Forest, and the Jemez Division of the Santa Fe Forest, his concern for the effects of human use increased. Meine records:

> This first public expression of his ideas on erosion came in an address entitled "Erosion and Prosperity," delivered January 18, 1921, during the observance of Farmer's Week at the University of Arizona … . Leopold recommended that the Prescott Forest personnel actively initiate artificial means of erosion control—check dams, willow planting, gully plugging—in specific problem areas.

Shortly after, his New Mexico Jemez inspection prompted a report of increased gullying:

> The range does not appear to be overstocked. Here again is an example to prove that erosion is inevitable on many ranges and cannot be checked except by artificial works. Many valuable *cienegas* are being drained by these gullies and the bottomland is being torn out (Meine, p. 186).

During his 1922 inspection of fire sites in the Gila Forest, Leopold took note of the deteriorating erosion problem there. His inspection report contained the initial Wilderness Area recommendation. And at the end of his tenure as operations manager in 1924, Leopold completed a *Watershed Handbook* that assembled all his previous work on the erosion problem, to teach field personnel how to diagnose and respond to watershed problems. In their 1995 compendium *Aldo Leopold's Southwest*,[21] Brown and Carmony reprinted Leopold's 1924 rigorous analysis and prevention article "Pioneers and Gullies," originally published in the popular *Sunset* magazine 52(5): 15-16, 91-95.

**Move To Wisconsin**

As we proceed forward carrying this record of early wilderness and land health events on our odyssey, let us maintain perspective for the evolving consciousness of a Land Ethic. In 1924, Aldo and Estella transferred from Albuquerque to Madison for an administrative position at the U.S. Forest Products Laboratory. Meine quotes a colleague saying that Leopold was a "fish out of water ... . We were scientists, engineers; Leopold was a forester" (p 234). Yet he goes on to describe:

> His conservationist convictions had always been, and would always remain, stronger than his social or political views and would ultimately subsume them. Leopold's beliefs about humankind's relationship to the natural world would expand to take in his beliefs about social relationships (Meine, p. 236).

The Leopold family had grown to five children, and in mid-career, he left the U.S. Forest Service on June 26, 1928, for a position conducting private game management surveys and worked independently as a consulting forester. His pioneering text *Game Management* was published in 1933.[22] That year he presented four major addresses in New Mexico. The University of Wisconsin then appointed him Professor of Game Management within the Department of Agricultural Economics, a unique position. His early work there included development of the new 500-acre Arboretum and Wildlife Refuge. At the dedication, Leopold said:

> It was not going to be just a collection of trees but a re-creation of the land as it once existed. It would be planted with entire plant communities: prairies, hardwood forest, coniferous forest, marsh (Meine, p. 328).

Likely inspired by these ideals, in January 1935, a day after his forty-eighth birthday, Leopold and a friend discovered a tract of abandoned farmland along the Wisconsin River. He bought the 80 acres for next to nothing. The only structure was an old chicken coop that the family converted to a bunkhouse and named "The Shack." Abbreviating the important story, this was the site of their restoration endeavors, phenology studies, and experiences that became the sources for *A Sand County Almanac*. This is also where Aldo suffered a fatal heart attack in 1948 fighting a neighbor's prairie fire.

A NEW MEXICO LAND ETHIC HANDBOOK

# Today's Land Ethic Institutions

Richard Rubin

## National Historic Registration

Mi Casita is the centerpiece of the National Historic Site registered as "The Old Tres Piedras Administrative Site of the Carson National Forest." This was done by Forest Service archaeologist Jon Nathan Young in 1991 and consists of seven buildings and five other structures scattered over an eight-acre area. The buildings are: House, Root Cellar, Barn, Shed, Oil House, and Cistern. The structures are: Barn Corral, Pole Corral, Stock Tank, Vehicle Yard, and Water Impoundment. We show photos and provide more details in our 2022 book *Living the Leopolds' Mi Casita Ecology*.[19] For our Land Ethic consciousness now, use historic imagination to consider how Leopold created a working compound with attention to environmental values and functional requirements. Archaeologist Jon Nathan Young stated in the National Register of Historic Places application:

> Leopold's experience in the Southwest—especially his field experience on the Carson at the Old Tres Piedras Administrative Site—was to guide his thinking ever after … . [It] is a memorial to the very beginnings of the National Forest Service and the American conservation ethic.

## Mi Casita Restoration

Government programs have also advanced the Land Ethic. Both political intention and funding were provided for the restoration of Mi Casita in honor of the U.S. Forest Service centennial in 2005. After the Leopolds, the house served as residence for many rangers and staff families. It was a Civilian Conservation Corps bunkhouse in the 1930s. Over the years, wooden windows had been changed to aluminum, beamed ceilings covered in panels, kitchen and bathroom cabinets remodeled, and the exterior painted institutional colors. The 2005 Aldo Leopold House Restoration and Rehabilitation Plan prepared by Recreation Solutions, A USDA Forest Service Enterprise Unit, states:

> Aldo Leopold, a principal founder of the modern conservationist movement, constructed his home on the Carson National Forest in 1912 … . When restored and rehabilitated, the house will function as a retreat for persons interested in modern conservation issues and as an interpretive site … . The Forest Service will offer the house to the public as a place of reflection and scholarly pursuits.

The plan detailed restoration back to the original appearance designed by Leopold in 1911–12. Period fixtures and furniture were installed, and the work was completed by 2007.[23]

**Our Current Mission in New Mexico**

Visitors now have opportunities for participation in various programs and resources available at Mi Casita. I shall briefly identify these with the intention to raise our conservation consciousness and continue creative evolution. In 2012, the Leopold Writing Program was organized in Albuquerque and began month-long residencies at Mi Casita "to foster Leopold's legacy of the written word exploring the relationship of nature and culture" (leopoldwritingprogram.org). To date, twenty-three professional writers, scholars, and journalists have participated. In addition, various student groups, from elementary to university levels, have come for tours and classes. The Forest Service conducts staff retreats for training and inspiration. Occasionally a visiting fire crew needs housing. Visitors are asked to leave guest-book messages, and their comments show the impact of Mi Casita experiences. Nearby Taos community groups such as the Native Plant Society and church congregations come to see the history and learn about our community's Land Ethic.

The Albuquerque Wildlife Federation which Aldo founded in 1914 continues public land and habitat rehabilitation projects. A group came to help with Mi Casita exterior painting and to witness installation of the National Historic Registration plaque in 2018. In our Introduction, I recognized their true spirit of the new Mi Casita mission, giving sixteen books by and about Leopold to establish a Forest Service library in memory of their University of New Mexico mentor Dr. Richard Becker. That library has now grown to 132 volumes from volunteer donations, publications by Writing Program residents, additions obtained from the Wisconsin Aldo Leopold Foundation, and retired ecology professionals supporting the ongoing scholarship.

**Establishing the Leopold Foundation in Wisconsin**

I depend here on Stephen Laubach's *Living a Land Ethic: A History of Cooperative Conservation on the Leopold Memorial Reserve.*[24] After Aldo's death, the family would visit and maintain the Shack and lands, particularly the children pursuing their educations as environmental scientists. Aldo's prior initiatives for regional landowner cooperative conservation were well known. In 1967, as contiguous and nearby landowners began recognizing threats of development, five families with a total of 900 acres agreed to a proposal of principles for the Leopold Memorial Preserve. Laubach records:

> Today [2014], the reserve has grown to over 1,600 acres that are overseen by two nonprofit organizations—the Sand County Foundation and the Aldo Leopold Foundation—with their roots in the Coleman and Leopold families … . Rather than pursuing government involvement, property owners of the reserve instead agreed to restrict development and cooperatively manage the land. In their case, they did so to honor the memory of Leopold, collectively putting into action his call for increased attention to conservation on private land (p. 5–6).

From 1968 through 1983, land management, research, and education programs grew under Preserve auspices. In 1982, the five Leopold children established a separate nonprofit organization, the Aldo Leopold Shack Foundation (ALSF). Their guiding principles:

> In particular, the ALSF focused more explicitly on the science, philosophy, and legacy of Aldo Leopold and less on the importance of conservation on private property … . The primary goals of the new foundation were (1) "to promote education and scientific research….designed to produce a sharper, deeper, broader, wiser vision of land and its use, and which may serve as a

> laboratory for the study of the wildlife and ecology of the area"; (2) "to promote for educational purposes the continued publication and public awareness of the scientific and literary works of Aldo Leopold"; and (3) "to perpetuate through such educational and scientific activities, the philosophies of conservation and custodianship of natural resources and to promote the practice of rehabilitation of land in order to return it to an approximation of its original pre-settlement condition, as such concepts were developed through the words and deeds of Aldo Leopold throughout his lifetime" (Laubach, p. 77).

Connecting to our Handbook theme:

> The work of the Bradleys [daughter Nina and husband Charlie] through their study center and of Starker, Luna, Carl, and Estella Leopold in writing management reports and contributing as board members of the Leopold Foundation indicated a clear preference for using the reserve as a center for ecological education and research efforts to foster an ecological conscience and land ethic (Laubach, p.77).

By 1995–1996, the programs and priorities of the Sand County Foundation and Aldo Leopold Foundation [having deleted Shack from its name] diverged. The SCF emphasis on private land stewardship continued. Based in Madison, they have expanded to water quality, soil health, and wildlife habitat programs, including Land Ethic mentorship for underserved ranchers and farmers nationally. Meanwhile, the ALF expanded its seminar program and provided tours of the Shack. In 1999, Wellington "Buddy" Huffaker became executive director and oversaw continuing growth. A new center for education, meetings, library, and offices was built in 2007 on contiguous property. Following Aldo's principles of living lightly on the land, it has earned the highest level in the U.S. Green Building Council's Leadership in Energy and Environmental Design (LEED) program.

Stephen Laubach concludes:

> The significance of the Shack property in conservation history radiated to other locations, and it also brought many visitors to the reserve from around the globe, especially after the opening of the Leopold Center in 2007. Those traveling to the reserve sought to understand the beauty of this unassuming landscape, where Aldo Leopold synthesized many of his ideas about conservation, land health, and environmental ethics (p. 94).

Paraphrasing from his Afterword:

> On the Leopold Memorial Reserve, this land, well on its way to recovery from the scars of poor agricultural practices, is an excellent example of the Land Ethic in action (p. 104).

The Foundation provides vital linking to the New Mexico legacy. My own opportunities for presence at Mi Casita introduced me to the migrating Sand Hill Cranes and Leopold Foundation teachings. Here is a piece I wrote for sharing with our community, reprinted from the *Taos News*, September 21, 2023:

### The Story of Sandhill Crane Restoration

The Aldo Leopold Foundation headquarters in Baraboo Wisconsin is reporting that cranes are now arriving at the nearby riverbanks on their annual migration south. When I am working at Mi Casita, I have watched large flights of greater sandhill cranes and heard their distinctive gurgling. Here's the story of why [columnist] Rick Romancito can now appreciate the "big, beautiful, and amazing pair of sandhill cranes spending a winter in Taos" (*Taos News Tempo,* August 17) while the large flocks usually prefer the Bosque del Apache National Wildlife Refuge we are all privileged to witness.

It is possible that the Leopolds saw flights of cranes migrating south along the Tusas Mountains during the Autumn of 1912. When appointed supervisor of the Carson National Forest, he built a Craftsman style bungalow as his headquarters and home for his new bride, Maria Alvira Estella Bergere from Santa Fe. Yet his near fatal storm exposure and kidney failure in April of 1913 forced a long recovery and their move to Albuquerque where Aldo continued in U.S. Forest Service administrative positions for ten years. As his values were evolving, Aldo's initiatives began to progress from hunting game management to wildlife conservation. He attempted preservation of the Middle Rio Grande Valley wetlands and developed the idea of wilderness protection for the Gila National Forest, eventually the first so designated by the Department of Agriculture.

However, it is also likely that Aldo and Estella did not experience the crane flocks' migration over Tres Piedras as the population was seriously declining. In 1924, they moved to Madison Wisconsin. After four years, he left the Forest Service and independently conducted wildlife surveys and conservation programs. Colleagues then organized a progressive opportunity for him at the University of Wisconsin as the first Professor of Game Management. Under his leadership, this evolved to Wildlife Management. His studies revealed that greater sandhill cranes had been nearly extirpated in the upper Midwest, meaning extinct from a particular area. Commercial market hunting overkill resulted in disappearance as a breeding bird from Illinois by 1890, Iowa by 1905, South Dakota by 1910, Ohio by 1926, and Indiana by 1929.

Some protection progress was conferred by the Migratory Bird Treaty with Canada in 1916 and the U.S. Migratory Bird Treaty Act of 1918. As described in his 1937 essay "Marshland Elegy," Leopold had minimal confidence that sandhill cranes would long survive despite their protection. He and his students surveyed the wetlands in the Sand Counties of central Wisconsin and reckoned there were just a few dozen cranes nesting in the 1930s. However, Stan Temple, University of Wisconsin Emeritus Professor and Senior Fellow at the Aldo Leopold Foundation, described in 2017 the 75,000 cranes then in the upper Great Lakes region and over 15,000 in Wisconsin. He pursued the issue of whether we should hunt them again:

"I suspect the cranes have achieved an elevated cultural value and that this now transcends their value as a renewable resource that could be exploited … . I imagine Aldo Leopold would have been thrilled by the sandhill crane's remarkable recovery … . I also suspect he would have been heartened to see that the debate has taken on an ethical dimension … . Once on the brink of extinction, the sandhill crane is now considered a symbol of hope, resiliency, and conservation success."

Consult www.aldoleopold.org for the resources, opportunities, and programs of today's Aldo Leopold Foundation. Or track down a copy of the elegant large *Almanac* edition with Shack and land photographs by Michael Sewell, Oxford University Press, 2001.

For this Handbook's mission, we return now to New Mexico to resume the Land Ethic trail. Shifting cultural consciousness and whetting your appetites, I provide a family tradition that Leopold's wife carried to Wisconsin.

In youngest daughter Estella B. Leopold's 2022 memoir *Aldo's Wife: Estella Bergere: My Remarkable Mother*, later life companion and home caretaker Alan Anderson relates her mother's beloved enchilada recipe.

### Estella's Enchiladas

Making 4 servings:

2 T. oil, 3 T. flour. Make a roux to golden color. Turn off the heat and add: 1 minced garlic clove, 4 T. Pure New Mexico chile powder (or to taste), Chimayo and Hatch brands are best.

After 30 seconds add: 2½ cups water, ½ teaspoon salt.

Return to heat and simmer 30 minutes. Can sit 'til ready to use; it's better the next day.

When ready to serve, reheat sauce. Have ready: 2 cups grated 2 year aged cheddar, 1 onion chopped 1/3 inch cubes, 8 corn tortillas.

Heat ½ inch of oil in 8 inch skillet over medium heat. When the oil sizzles when tortilla is added, it is ready.

For each plate: Fry one tortilla in oil for ten seconds, flip for 10 seconds more, then place on pre-heated plate. Top with grated cheese and onion and ¼ c. sauce. Repeat with second layer and serve immediately with a side of beans that have been soaked overnight and cooked until soft (op. cit., p. 125).

# Modern
## Wilderness Encounters
### Richard Rubin

This Handbook is a collection of stories based on human experiences following Leopold's insights and practices. Many comprehensive guidebooks and maps are available for wilderness exploration. But I intend to go beyond named places, seeking the inherent values for ethical relationship to *The Land* following Leopold's inclusive definition. Early political arguments for wilderness called for preservation for science's sake. Arthur Carhart sought an aesthetic resource for future generations to enjoy. Leopold in 1921 argued for recreational opportunities. His definition then said:

> By "wilderness" I mean a continuous stretch of country preserved in its natural state, open to lawful hunting and fishing, big enough to absorb a two weeks' pack trip, and kept devoid of roads, artificial trails, cottages, or other works of man.[25]

In debating those who primarily sought economic benefits from the forests, Leopold recognized the additional cultural value, "wealth to the human spirit." Here is a personal reflection I wrote for the *Taos News*, July 2, 2022, when the book *First and Wildest* was introduced:

### Honoring the Gila Wilderness

The importance of our American wilderness areas has evolved despite many controversies and deserves enhanced attention now on the one hundredth anniversary of establishing the Gila Wilderness. This first is a New Mexico story. It goes beyond politics to be rightly regarded a century later as a powerful enhancement of the ongoing ecological relationship to our land. Aldo Leopold is credited with inspiring the certification of this first Federally protected wilderness. After his near-death kidney failure suffered on Jicarilla District range patrol in 1913, the Leopolds lived and worked in Albuquerque for ten years. Scholars have credited this time as valuable for Aldo's emerging transition from Forestry to Conservation, including protection of our public lands.

What do I think is important for the Taos community to consider now? First, in recognizing this centennial of the Gila Wilderness establishment, an important book of essays was just released: *First and Wildest: The Gila Wilderness at 100,* from Torrey House Press, 2022.[26] Twenty-five contributors describe meaningful experiences with the Gila Wilderness.

## MODERN WILDERNESS ENCOUNTERS

Quoting the Introduction:

"We have gathered members of that community [a reference to Leopold's statement "It evolves in the minds of a thinking community"] in the pages that follow. They include politicians, poets, biologists, biographers, horsepackers and fire lookouts, archaeologists and administrators. They are Anglo, Apache, Mexican American, and all of the above. And the Gila means different things to each of them (p. x)."

Second, we should be aware that attitudes and practices about wilderness areas range among preservation passion, multi-use government policies, political conflict over commercial exploitation, controversy over indigenous and historic culture rights, wildlife extinction, and criticism of recreational abuse by the ecologically entitled.

Third, in addition to these complex issues, there are personal values wilderness can provide us. As naturalized first-generation New Mexicans, Annette and I have memories of our own meaningful experiences in the Gila Wilderness that move us to honor this centennial and Aldo Leopold's wisdom. We met in June of 1968, coming independently after Eastern college graduations for health care and education program service in Arizona and New Mexico. We moved to Albuquerque in 1972 when I was accepted to a medical internship at the University of New Mexico Hospitals. Two weeks before beginning work, we jeeped for backpacking to the Gila Wilderness.

Like many of the essay writers in *First and Wildest,* we each had unexpected and influential experiences there. I remember finding a girl from a nearby ranch and her mother after the child fell off her horse and suffered an upper arm fracture. I had learned the correct way to stabilize a fractured arm with a sling from our kit. The mother and daughter were relieved, and so was I when a Forest Service truck pulled up. This was a maturing experience for me, realizing my transition from medical student to responsible Good Samaritan physician.

We then hiked a few miles inside the wilderness boundary from a trailhead and set up camp by one of the Gila River tributaries. Annette sought interesting photographs, especially of wildflowers. I was developing my fly-fishing skills and was excited to pursue wild trout. I explored upstream one sunny morning. An hour became several, and Annette came looking for me, worried that I was injured. She was very glad to find me just happily engrossed in fishing. Her own maturing experience was realizing the possibilities when alone in the wilderness. Her anxiety evolved to awareness that adventures included risks, that she could walk out to our vehicle, and that search and rescue efforts for me were possible. She felt confident in her resilience. I think such life events are among the values of wilderness. Beyond the philosophical, recreational, and land ethic justifications for wilderness protection, we are grateful for the personal memories. And glad they can be written about now in our later years.

Feeling honored that my own life with Annette in New Mexico can even vaguely approach the qualities of Estella and Aldo, I share this story from daughter Estella's recent memoir *Aldo's Wife Estella Bergere: My Remarkable Mother* (op. cit.). Her mother Estella is conversing with Alan Anderson, a graduate student who served as her companion and home caretaker in later years. He writes in the memoir:

> Once [when reminiscing about Aldo] she smiled a huge smile and asked me, "Do you know what we did on our honeymoon?" "No," I replied.
>
> "We rode horses into the mountains and set up a base camp. We spent the days hunting and fishing. We would read books out loud to each other and write in our journals. One day Aldo went out hunting by himself in the afternoon. I stayed in camp and read. It started to get late, later than the time he said he would be back. I began to get worried, and as the light began to fade, he came back. I was very relieved, and as he approached me, he had his hands behind his back. With a big grin, he asked what I thought he had behind him.

And do you know what it was?" "No, what was it?" I asked.

"It was the liver of a deer. He had shot a deer and had dressed and hung it to retrieve the next day, but he had brought the liver back to camp for a late dinner! It was such fun! Just wonderful!" (p.151).

I like to think our experiences express the values described by Philip Cafaro:

> Thoreau, Leopold, and Carson provide inspiring accounts of human beings living well in nature. They suggest to me the rudiments of an environmental virtue ethics that is noble and challenging and makes room for the rest of creation. To arguments for preserving nature in our own materialistic self-interest and arguments for preserving nature for its intrinsic value, they add arguments for preserving nature in order to preserve human possibilities and help us become better people. That such arguments may convince and inspire is proven by these authors' enduring popularity and by their roles in shaping modern environmental consciousness (Cafaro, p. 39).

Similarly, Roderick Nash in *Wilderness and the American Mind*[27] quotes Leopold's view that the wilderness preservation movement was:

> A disclaimer of the biotic arrogance of *homo americanus.* It is one of the focal points of a

new attitude—an intelligent humility toward
man's place in nature … . The richest values of
wilderness lie not in the days of Daniel Boone,
nor even in the present, but rather in the future
("Wilderness Values" in *Living Wilderness,* 7
(1942).[28]

Leeanna Torres describes herself as a native daughter of the American Southwest, a *Nuevomexicana* who has worked as an environmental professional—from fish biologist to natural resources specialist- throughout the West since 2001. She was a Leopold Writing Program resident at Mi Casita in 2014. Her essay "Goyahkla" [the original name for Geronimo] appears in the *First and Wildest* collection. She wrote:

> The Gila Wilderness is as large and expansive as an ocean. It is over five hundred thousand acres of undisturbed forest land, most of it unaccustomed to the blunt interruptions of human society. No stores, no streetlights, no roads, no eighteen-wheelers. There is only the rawness of the earth, in all its beauty and terror. The only sounds are the birds, the water, the shuffling wildlife, your own fearful heartbeat when you realize just how far you are from civilization.
>
> Like so many things in our spectacular, amazing, privileged American life, I take "wilderness" for granted. I take the national parks, the federal forest system, the designated wilderness areas, all for granted. Of course, there was great controversy,

> battle, struggles for their creation, but they exist now, and they are a part of our heritage. Bold, brave, even arrogant men had the insight to create these areas for *us,* the American public. But was it *taken* or was it *preserved*? Was it *stolen* or was it *designated*? Geronimo [said to have been born in these mountains] and his Chiricahua Apache comrades finally surrendered to U.S. troops in 1886. Goyahkla was forced to live out his life at Fort Sill, Oklahoma, where he was considered a tourist attraction (p. 102–3, italics by Leeanna).

## Pecos Happenings

When Annette and I moved from St. Louis to Albuquerque in 1972 to begin my medical internship at the University of New Mexico Hospitals, we bought a basic house in the northwest corner of Bernalillo County. In those years before Rio Rancho suburbs and shopping center sprawl, our land was open to the west mesa and in view of Sandia Peak across the North Valley. The previous owner had built a corral and sturdy small stable. We soon acquired grade saddle horses for exploring; Annette a roan Appaloosa named Sandia and I a pinto retired barrel racer named Chato. Horses were familiar because our main recreation during medical school and teaching job stresses in St Louis was a cooperative venture with friends to support riding steeds at a barn in the woods 20 miles from the city.

Different from our past woodland adventures, outdoor sports, and camp life in the East and Midwest, the New Mexico wilderness areas were intriguing. Here are a few stories of where we explored, what we encountered, how we learned, and the effects on our characters. You've learned in the above essay about our early trip to the Gila. Being small to average size people, we decided backpacking was too strenuous, so we planned trips trailering the horses behind our jeep. We were enthusiastic about the view of Bob Marshall, a provocative early wilderness advocate, as quoted in a recent Aldo Leopold Foundation Newsletter for "seeking inspiration, aesthetic enjoyment, and a gain in understanding."

The mystique of the Pecos Wilderness was inspiring then, the mountain views appealing, and new adventure enticing. And it was the closest wilderness drive from our Alameda home trailering the two horses. Our first excursion was a day ride in from a base campground with corrals. From that experience, we planned a three-day trip with a Santa Fe couple, nurse and dentist friends from Indian Health Service days. We surely had conditioning and health contingencies well covered. They hired saddle and pack horses from a local outfitter in Pecos. Yup, Bob Marshall would have been pleased with our gumption. But I learned some land ethic lessons, at least in that summer when snow was still melting up high. However well trained for home riding, our typical saddle horses did not have trail horse qualities. They balked at the several small streams crossing the trail, so extra coaxing was required. Next lesson: the horses were hobbled appropriately overnight in the meadow where we camped. However, in the morning I disliked the degree of damage they did, trampling the fragile native plants. Yes, we were relative greenhorns, but with the right consciousness, we learned with a land ethic attitude.

Afterwards, we limited trail rides to short trailer trips and excursions from home. In those days before the North Valley and West Mesa building boom, we could ride to the Rio Grande bosque. The horses liked that better, too. Meine reports that Aldo took son Starker there for a dove hunt on his tenth birthday (p. 218).

So doing some research and trying to think like a wilderness area, I decided to go more traditional and obtain a burro. A newspaper ad led me to a field in the Manzano mountains for the jack we named *Orejo Rojo*. He was medium-sized and mostly grey with rusty ears. As living in community with all creatures is an ethic virtue, we welcomed him. He turned out to have a sociable personality and appeared to enjoy his lean-to shed next to the horse stalls, including the company of barnyard chickens. One of Rojo's quirks was braying at dawn with the rooster, but no neighbors complained up

on our mesa edge. By no means dumb and stubborn, Rojo definitely had his own mind regarding human expectations.

As more wilderness adventures called us, I assembled Rojo's outfit. But first, in the spirit of Aldo's scholarship, I did some homework. I still have three informative books. The first is a comprehensive text by Frank Brookshier from Maxwell New Mexico, *The Burro,* University of Oklahoma Press, 1974. The second is a little manual *Going Light with Backpack or Burro: How to Get Along on Wilderness Trails (Chiefly in the West),* Sierra Club 1968. And the most useful was *Horses, Hitches, and Rocky Trails* by Joe Back, Swallow Press, 1959. The flyleaf description alerts: "The wilderness is no place for the person who doesn't know what he is doing. The reader will be better equipped for the wilderness than he was before reading it. It is *that kind* of truly helpful book."

Despite my teenage nature camp and fishing experience, I learned much more about knot and cinch tying. Next, Dan's Boots and Saddles store on NW Fourth St had a traditional Sawbuck pack saddle to sell me. I then built two sturdy pannier boxes with hinged lids, curved inner side, and rope handles for hanging on the cross trees. They were rodent proof for food storage and provided seats around the campfire. That is, except at night when we hung them out of ursine reach. The load was completed with a duffel bag for clothes, sleeping bags, tent, etc., tied on top with a rain tarp cover secured by a cross hitch. Loaded, Rojo carried about sixty pounds that greatly relieved me and Annette. We could even bring a cast iron skillet for trout frying.

So prepared, we reprised the Pecos trip with our friends on foot. Rojo loaded the borrowed horse trailer fine after negotiating for a handful of sweetfeed. On the trail, he fulfilled his species' reputation for being sure-footed and cooperative crossing streams. At night when hobbled in the meadow, he did much less environmental damage than the horses. One final anecdote from the return trail: Annette and friend Mary were walking ahead carrying small daypacks. A pair of young guys with big packs were resting by the trail, and complained to the ladies that they heard weird noises at dawn. Then they noticed the small packs and asked, "Did you all camp out?" Their query was answered as I ambled down the trail, leading fully packed Rojo. We explained about his dawn braying habit. There is much to learn in the wilderness.

## Jemez Mountains' San Pedro Parks Wilderness

While we reached the Pecos driving northeast from Alameda, the Santa Fe National Forest to the northwest included the Jemez Mountains and San Pedro Parks Wilderness. We gave Rojo some relief from pack burdens and took him for light exploring trips. But first, I want to tell you about the efficiency of our travel adaptations. Becoming annoyed at the clunky mechanics of our '71 Jeep Commando, a hodgepodge of parts from the Willys Company bankruptcy then, I had traded it for a '74 Ford Ranger pickup. With some woodworking tools and free weekend time from internship duties, I built a frame for the truck bed with a rear door that came down to make a ramp. Negotiating as usual for a sweetfeed treat, Rojo would amble up. We received many smiles as we rode around with him back there. So we took a few day trips to the Jemez, camped at the Parks Wilderness edge, and hiked in to explore, leading him with minimal load of ponchos and lunch.

San Pedro Parks had limited tourist pressure, being further from the Soda Dam and Battleship Rock sights and the popular Jemez River trout stream. In June 1920, Leopold had inspected the area, particularly the forest lands adjacent to the Rio de Las Vacas with headwaters in the Park. Note from the name, this was an active cattle grazing area. His report indicated recent signs of increased erosion gullying, but he concluded that the range does not appear to be overstocked (Meine, p. 186). I was curious to evaluate the cutthroat trout fishing potential there. German brown trout stocked in the lower river decades ago had become wild and encroached on the natives' habitat. Entering the designated wilderness space impressed the idea that we too were visitors, trying not to be exploiters. While Rojo's distant equine ancestors had a North American presence, feral horses and burros were not overgrazing there to compete with livestock and wild ungulates. But they do in the northern section of the Carson Jicarilla District, around the area where Leopold had his harsh weather exposure. One of the Mi Casita historic structures is a holding corral, and in recent years a trio of these wild horses has been offered for public adoption. But no burros, much as I fancy having one in the family again.

**Living in Sight of Wilderness:
Wheeler Peak and the Columbine-Hondo**

The home we built in 1992 is north of Taos town, just outside the old village of Arroyo Seco. We look out straight east onto El Salto Peak, which is largely Carson National Forest. This continues up and to the south until the border of Taos Pueblo land at Pueblo Peak, popularly called Taos Mountain. A high ridge runs from Taos Ski Valley to Wheeler Peak, the highest in New Mexico at 13,161 feet. Herbert Ungnade's *A Guide to the New Mexico Mountains* [29] described multiple jeep roads going past the old Twining mine and across Bull O' the Woods Meadow. We took the pickup of Drew and Mary Turner (our Pecos adventure friends) there in 1973, and the rough ride taught us that's not smart mountaineering. Wheeler Peak had designation as a Wild Area of 6,051 acres in 1960, then that became a Wilderness Area in 1964 after new Federal legislation. The protected area was expanded to 14,700 acres in 1980 when the New Mexico Wilderness Act was passed, the end of any more vehicle intrusions.

There is more to the story than bureaucratic history, and it represents our changing opportunities for relationship to this important land. Yes, this was further evolution in our Land Ethic community qualities. Our many experiences have been diverse. We see the clouds and winds on 12,600-foot Lake Fork Peak from home, the southwestern boundary of Taos Ski Valley. More than just a map border, when up there skiing the ridge, we could look down on (but not enter) the area of sacred Blue Lake, restored by the Forest Service to the Pueblo in 1973.

The most popular hiking trail in Taos County goes to Williams Lake from the Kachina Peak base area of the Ski Valley into the Wheeler Wilderness. We have hiked it numerous times, always a different encounter. The change of consciousness, if you are so attuned, comes a half mile in with a sign declaring the wilderness boundary. The trail then proceeds two miles further and ascends one thousand feet to the lake lying at the base of Wheeler Peak. Wildlife opportunities include marmots, pikas, elk, mule deer, and golden eagles. Bighorn sheep had been extirpated by hunting but were restored about twenty years ago. This is another addition to our theme of evolution in relationship to the land as Leopold prophesied. I know people who do this hike each month of the year.

Back in 1995, the hike to Wheeler Peak took all day coming from the Ski Valley at Bull O' the Woods meadow, across the ridges, then down a steep trail of scree to the lake.

I did one such adventure with my son, then fifteen. The risk in summer was afternoon lightning storms, about the worst danger when exposed up there. Eight years ago, the Forest Service cut a new trail of moderate degree switchbacks between Williams Lake and the Wheeler summit. Enabling human access can be good, with the right conduct and agency stewardship.

Turning our attention northeast, the Carson Forest begins about three fourths mile from our house. The boundary sign stands at the beginning of the Rio Hondo Canyon and the road leads eight miles towards and two thousand feet up to the Taos Ski Valley base area. The Carson Forest designations on the north side of the road have evolved in our several decades. There are four marked trails along this section of Highway 150, called the Ski Valley Road: in order heading north, Yerba, Manzanita, Italianos, and Gavilan. These have fascinating stories well described elsewhere, as in Cindy Brown's *Taos Hiking Guide*. These ascents all lead up to the Long Canyon trail that continues north to Gold Hill. Years ago, we encountered grazing cows on Manzanita, but none recently. Each trail provides a different experience with multiple stream crossings and steepness among the mixed conifers and aspens. From Study Area status, the Columbine-Hondo area was designated permanent wilderness in 2015. The trails are popular year-round with locals and tourists. The wildflower displays are special. The opportunity is part of our consciousness as we consider when to go, pending the weather, ice, run off, autumn glory, and so on. Anytime, our dogs love it. They know it is a distinctive forest. And in the place we call home.

While I have related stories of our learning experiences in New Mexico wilderness, this is not always a "do it yourself" necessity. The U.S. Forest Service Southwest Region has recently prepared an informative practical fold-out guide titled *Back-Country Ethics*. And the National Wilderness Preservation System[31] developed the website wilderness.net "providing online resources for wilderness stewardship." The

NWPS was established to "secure for the American people of present and future generations the benefits of enduring wilderness resources." This partnership project includes the Arthur Carhart National Wilderness Training Center and the Aldo Leopold Wilderness Research Institute.

This last paragraph of Leopold's essay "Wilderness" precedes "The Land Ethic" in *A Sand County Almanac:*

> Ability to see the cultural value of wilderness boils down, in the last analysis, to a question of intellectual humility. The shallow-minded modern who has lost his rootage in the land assumes he has already discovered what is important; it is such who prate of empires, political or economic, that will last a thousand years. It is only the scholar who appreciates that all history consists of successive excursions from a single starting point to which man returns again and again to organize yet another search for a durable scale of values. It is only the scholar who understands why the raw wilderness gives definition and meaning to the human enterprise (op. cit., p. 189).

A modern view of such humility was expressed by Scott Russell Sanders in *A Conservation Manifesto.*[32]

> The Sabbath and the wilderness remind us of what is true everywhere and at all times, but which in our arrogance we keep forgetting—that we did not make the earth, that we are guests here, that we are answerable to a reality deeper and older and more sacred than our own will (p. 167).

# Gila
## Wilderness Complexity
### Andrew Gulliford

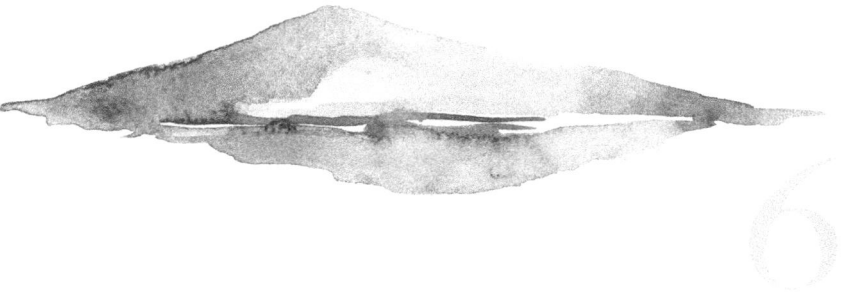

On Colorado's Western Slope in the small town of Silt, I started my forty-year teaching career when Silt still had dirt streets and wooden waterlines. I taught fourth grade and collected oral histories from folks who had survived the Great Depression. They in turn taught me to hunt for mule deer and elk, and I learned the difference between the White River National Forest, the second oldest in the nation, and the Flat Tops Wilderness with its dozens of high-altitude lakes. I came to understand that the wilderness idea of a landscape devoid of roads and structures had been proposed by landscape architect Arthur Carhart, the first such career professional hired after World War I by the U.S. Forest Service. The idea of setting aside land to be undisturbed came from Arthur Carhart and one summer he spent at Trappers Lake in 1919.

At Fort Lewis College in Durango, Colorado, I teach a popular class titled "American Wilderness" where students learn about wilderness as an idea, an ideal, and a law. The Pilgrims, looking at the vast forests of New England, claimed that the Atlantic Coast harbored "savage beasts and savage men." They were terrified of wild country and sought to re-create the pastoral landscape of Europe. George F. Will writes that the American experiment with democracy began as "an errand into the wilderness." We meant to tame the land.

Slowly a conservation ethic emerged. By 1890 the frontier had ended and astute Americans began to understand that if we developed the entire American continent we would lose something essential to our own character. Unlike any other nation, American philosophy, institutions and ideas have been shaped by our contact with wild land.

Congress created the National Park Service in 1916 and the U.S. Forest Service, established in 1905, became concerned about losing acreage to national parks and began to develop recreation areas. A young landscape architect, Arthur Carhart, was dispatched to Trappers Lake to survey the lake shore for summer cabins that would be built on leased land. Luckily, Carhart did more fishing than surveying. One evening after Pennsylvania fishermen admonished him to leave the lake alone, he walked back to his campsite and had an epiphany.

He wrote,

> Here, as I loafed along the trail, was a place, a moment, when one could explore his thoughts. Suddenly a strange sibilance filled the basin. I halted. I listened. The soft eerie whispers came clearly through the sun-drenched air. I glanced in all directions, hoping to discover their source. I failed. Silence returned quickly. Abruptly the strange sound returned, increased, dimmed, and in a moment was gone.

I've studied Carhart's papers at the Denver Public Library and over the years I've come to believe that as he walked the Trappers Lake perimeter trail, he was visited by a Ute spirit. Carhart had experienced a moment of revelation and realized that the shoreline of Trappers Lake should not be marred by tourist cabins. Prior to that time no government official had conceived of leaving land in its natural state. The concept of protecting wilderness areas in national forests was thus born on ancient Ute lands.

Thomas Wolf has written the definitive biography of Carhart titled *Arthur Carhart: Wilderness Prophet*.[7] Wolf quotes Carhart about the landscape architect's summer at Trappers Lake:

> As I roughed out the survey on which access roads would be located and cottage lots plotted, I began to feel uneasy. The place was getting a strange hold on me. I experienced a quality of peace, exhilaration at being a part of it. The spirit and values of wilderness would be ruptured and rent when the lake was girdled with little buildings, autos rambled back and forth on a shoreline road and motorboats chattered across the lake. I liked Trappers without these distractions.

Ute elders agree that Trappers Lake had a "strange hold" on the young man and that yes, he "experienced a quality of peace" at one of their sacred sites. They think that Native American guardian spirits spoke directly to Carhart. Because of the spirits' soft voices Trappers Lake is now known as the cradle of the American wilderness movement—land without roads or development where "man is a visitor who does not remain." Later Carhart shared his thoughts with the regional forester in Denver. Another young forester sat in on that meeting. Aldo Leopold would take Carhart's idea and implement it in southwest New Mexico creating the Gila Wilderness in 1924—the first such wilderness in the world. Forty years later Congress would pass federal legislation to create a wilderness preservation system. For years the law was stuck in a Congressional committee.

As a nineteenth century conservation movement evolved into a twentieth century environmental movement, groups campaigned for federal wilderness and Howard Zahniser of the Wilderness Society wrote a bill to create a national wilderness preservation system. Congressman Wayne Aspinall from Colorado was not amused. An old-style conservationist who believed in utilizing all natural resources, Aspinall never met a dam he didn't like. He feared that the wilderness bill would "lock up" resources so he forced sixty-six re-writes. Each time the wording got better and the legislation came to focus on two key points: grazing would be continued in wilderness and only Congress could legally designate wilderness areas.

Environmentalists bristle over cows in pristine areas, but they should admire Aspinall for what he did. By refusing to let federal agencies designate wilderness and demanding that only Congress had that right, Aspinall inadvertently gave birth to the modern environmental movement in which dispersed local groups rally their members to protect public lands and influence Congress. Without knowing it, Aspinall deepened and broadened the environmental movement because the 1964 Wilderness Act requires citizen involvement.

I've hiked up the Chinese Wall at Trappers Lake. As youthful, energetic backpackers my wife and I left our VW camper bus in the parking lot and trekked into the Flat Tops Wilderness. We had a terrifying night of rain and lightning. I forgot utensils so we ate macaroni and cheese first with sticks and then with our fingers. We got wet. We made mistakes. We were forced to become more resourceful, and we did.

I treasure those memories and that's why I'm never as happy as when I step across a wilderness boundary. Once across that magical border I know that I will encounter only hikers or horseback riders because motorized vehicles and mountain bikes are not allowed. Behind me is a world of machines and roads and ahead a landscape as wild as any that can be found in America. Now the Wilderness Act has had its fiftieth anniversary and it was Aldo Leopold who first implemented wilderness ideals.

Trapper's Lake is now considered the Cradle of Wilderness. Leopold took Carhart's idea of leaving the landscape alone and implemented it with designation of the Gila Wilderness. Having backpacked and climbed into the Flat Tops Wilderness, I then met Leopold's vision on his own turf in southwest New Mexico. Later in my career, I directed the Western New Mexico University Museum in Silver City. In cooperation with the Gila National Forest, we decided to have an exhibit on the meaning and value of wilderness. In the museum's files I found an extraordinary original document, a primary source. We had a typed copy of Leopold's memo recommending the Gila as wilderness. At only two and a half pages, the manuscript elucidated Leopold's thoughts in his clear, precise prose. This was the Declaration of Independence for the wilderness concept, and we proudly put it on display.

Hikes into the Gila and teaching university classes on wilderness continued to impact my thinking and drew me closer to Leopold and his prescient vision. As I came to know the Gila, I came to know myself and to better understand the Land Ethic that is the seminal purpose of this book.

One of the least visited and most pristine environments in the United States is in the mountains of southwest New Mexico. Here, where the Continental Divide stretches north from Mexico, a spectacular country of canyons, hot springs, mesas, and mountaintops survives as an ecological island: the 800,000-acre Gila and Aldo Leopold wildernesses, within the 3.3 million-acre Gila National Forest. From Sonoran Desert and exotic cactus below to spruce, fir, and aspen above,

rising to 10,892 feet at the summit of Whitewater Baldy, the Gila River region is rich in biological and cultural diversity. But it is the wilderness itself which survives as a truly unique ecosystem, though Mexican wolves are struggling.[8]

Set aside in 1924 as the nation's first designated wilderness, the Gila Wilderness is both a physical reality and the culmination of a distinctly American ideal to preserve a landscape and an environment in its original unspoiled condition. Yet even the Gila is not as natural as it seems. In 1909, after graduating from Yale with a master's degree in forestry, young Aldo Leopold headed to the mountains of Arizona and New Mexico. He hunted, fished and surveyed on horseback this forest domain. All the while, he observed where human encroachments had resulted in the land getting portioned into mere vestiges of what was once a true wilderness. He called these patches "tag-ends" of the once boundless American landscape and "fly-specks on the map." An erudite philosopher and creative thinker who helped invent the concepts of wild ecology and wildlife management, he wanted all Americans to experience the awesome space that had overwhelmed the first Western pioneers.[9]

To say that Aldo Leopold was ahead of his time is an understatement. He understood the human need for solitude and sanctuary. In *A Sand County Almanac* he would eloquently argue, "Of what avail are forty freedoms without a blank spot on the map?" In 1924 Leopold's wilderness proposal was accepted by the Southwest regional office of the U.S. Forest Service, but there was still no federal law protecting roadless areas nor was there a Congressionally accepted philosophy on wilderness and the value of wild landscapes.

Although three quarters of a million acres had been set aside as a "primitive area," white settlement had already occurred deep within it along the forks of the Gila River. Until the Great Depression of the 1930s collapsed farm prices, Anglo settlers and Hispanic farmers were earning a meager living in the Gila's isolated canyons and narrow river valleys. Gradually, the settlers drifted away, as had the prehistoric Mimbres Indians who had lived in the same valleys. The U.S. Forest Service had owned the mountain-sides; now, thanks to unpaid property taxes, it gradually began to own the river bottoms.

In the mid-1920s, the Forest Service drafted "L-20 Regulations" to keep primitive areas wild with regard to "environment, transportation, habitation, and subsistence." However, the "primitive" designation did not include protections

for wildlife. The federal government continued to carry out its predator control policy of hiring bounty hunters to shoot mountain lions, grizzly bears, and wolves. In 1931, the last grizzly in the Southwest wandered out of the Gila Wilderness and was shot to death by a rancher.

During the Depression, the Civilian Conservation Corps (CCC) came to the Gila National Forest and the Gila Wilderness. The CCC workers built some of the first trails into the wilderness, making progress toward Leopold's vision. They also created the first campgrounds outside the wilderness. These campgrounds, merely level places in the woods without facilities, were built adjacent to the new North Star Road, completed in 1934, which connected the Mimbres River Valley with Beaverhead Ranger Station. The North Star Road split the Gila Wilderness into two wildernesses, with the Gila to the west and the Aldo Leopold Wilderness to the east. This dirt and gravel road, known today as New Mexico 61 and the Outer Loop, bisected the wilderness to create access for fire control and into the northern part of the vast forest, "but with due regard to the preservation of wilderness values."

World War II brought an end to the CCC and to mining camps near the wilderness areas. Towns that supported them, like Mogollon and Graham, began to wither. With few men to hunt, game populations multiplied. The end of WWII resulted in a surplus of Jeeps. Because they were accessible to all Americans, it didn't take long for the use of the rugged four-wheel-drive vehicles to expose a flaw in the wisdom of Aldo Leopold's plan for a roadless wilderness area. The vast Gila National Forest, home to elk, mule deer, mountain lions, javelina, and wild turkey, became a hunter's paradise. Hunters used Jeeps to make their own roads, and because no guidelines had been established for wilderness management, the Forest Service also accessed wilderness using Jeeps, tractors and even small airplanes. Though the Gila received protection in 1924, few rules or regulations existed for the wilderness, and no regulations restricted miners from building Jeep trails to their remote mining claims.

In 1952, the Southwest Regional Forester suggested reducing the area of the wilderness to open Iron Creek Mesa to lumbering, prior to transferring the reserve to permanent wilderness status under the new U-1 Regulation. A full third of the wilderness was on the chopping block. Silver City, New Mexico citizens balked and formed an unlikely coalition to fight the plan. Gathered for the fight were the Sierra Club, the American Legion, the Lions Club, the

Chamber of Commerce, and sportsmen's organizations. The group succeeded, serving notice to the Forest Service that the Gila Wilderness should not be reduced in size. Then in 1964, with passage of the Wilderness Act, national legislation set specific guidelines on wilderness use and created new challenges for the Gila's district rangers.

The 1964 Wilderness Act proclaimed, "a wilderness…is hereby recognized as an area where the earth and community of life are untrammeled by man, where man himself is a visitor who does not remain." But humans had been living in the Gila Wilderness for the last thousand years. With the Act's passage, zealous Forest Service employees burned historic corrals and log cabins that may have endured as valuable cultural resources. While the Forest Service sought to return the wilderness to its natural state, angry four-wheelers sought to test the new law.

A four-wheel-drive club from El Paso, Texas arrived to drive their Jeeps through the Gila River and into the wilderness. Stalled in unexpected flood waters, the Jeeps were abandoned. Later, when club members petitioned the Forest Service to permit them to retrieve their stuck vehicles and drive them out of the wilderness, the Gila responded with a steadfast "no." The Jeep owners had to pay dearly to have mules pull out their vehicles.

Despite the demise of grizzly bears and limited numbers of Mexican wolves, plant and animal life has thrived in the Gila. Today the Mexican Spotted Owl, a small cousin of the Northern Spotted Owl that in the 1980s headlined threatened species in the Northwest, lives quietly among thick stands of ponderosa pine. Biological survey teams have sought out the reclusive owls as part of a baseline study of the owl's nocturnal travels.

The Gila River Valley is the only known home for the endangered spikedace and loach minnows. The Sonoran mountain king snake, the narrowhead garter snake, and the Gila trout are also endangered species as are plants like grama grass cactus, grayish white giant hyssop, Mogollon whitlow grass, the threadleaf false carrot, and the Pinos Altos flamethrower.[10] Raptors abound, including a variety of hawks, eagles and ubiquitous turkey vultures. During the Great Depression of the 1930s, New Mexico's Fish and Game Department introduced game trout into the Gila's streams. But the rainbows, cutthroats and German browns came to dominate the natural habitat of the native Gila trout, which led to its listing as an endangered species a half century later. After years of complicated fish studies and a careful reintroduction plan, biologists thought they were looking at a success story.

At one point they even considered downgrading the Gila trout from endangered status to threatened. But all the efforts and a carefully executed reintroduction program were washed away in a week of heavy rains coming on the heels of massive forest fires in the late 1980s. Silt and dirt washing into remote Gila streams clogged the gills of the rare fish, and they suffocated and died. Dazed and disappointed, but undaunted, teams of biologists reintroduced Gila trout into other creeks.[11]

Cattle grazing has been one of the most controversial issues of contemporary wilderness management and creates conundrums for implementation of Leopold's Land Ethic, which stresses biological diversity. A Congressional compromise in the 1964 Wilderness Act authorizes cattle in wilderness areas where grazing had been historically practiced.[12] It is believed that the presence of cattle in wilderness has altered natural vegetation patterns and destroyed communities of plants. Alligator-juniper trees are now in close proximity to ponderosa pine habitat. The pinon-juniper advance, known by range and conservation staff as the "PJ invasion," may be the result of extensive overgrazing in the Gila.

Since the early 1900s, the number and range of grassy meadows in the Gila has been reduced, along with the ability of native grasses to sustain wildfires because the grasses are no longer naturally thick and luxuriant. They've been cropped short by grazing. Also, a dearth of grasses and a misguided Forest Service fire suppression policy begun in 1910 changed the natural cycles of fire and plant rebirth.[13] Fires burn as part of the natural process in the Gila ecosystem, but excessive dry years and large out of control fires altered fire ecology in the Gila. Fire managers were often prohibited from allowing fires to safely burn naturally in the Gila Wilderness. "Prescribed burns" may mitigate the problem, but the fuel wood cycle is off balance. In some areas of the Gila there is too much downed wood from previous fires to let a fire burn "naturally" without creating a catastrophe.[14]

The Mogollon Rim, which stretches a wild, ragged line across Arizona to New Mexico, has one of the highest incidents of lightning-caused fires in the world. On one June night in 1989, more than 3,000 lightning strikes hit the Gila National Forest. By dawn ninety fires were ablaze. Because wilderness regulations restrict mechanized equipment, firefighters and smokejumpers are challenged to access the Mogollon's steep canyons and uneven terrain. But they have adjusted. Fire management techniques now include rappelling out of helicopters into fire zones.

By the 1970s, visitor usage of the Gila Wilderness had increased dramatically. And in one case, massively. In 1977, the Rainbow Family of Living Light applied for a permit to hold its annual Rainbow Gathering in the East Fork of the Gila. The permit was granted, despite the probability of severe resource damage, and five thousand members of the Rainbow family converged to camp in a quiet side canyon of the Gila. A baby was born during the event and died there. He and countless Native Americans, early settlers and former U.S. Cavalry soldiers are buried in unmarked graves in the wilderness.

Unscrupulous opportunists found in the Gila a land of opportunity as grave robbers. On benches above the Gila's flood line, the prehistoric Mimbres Indians had left their dead buried in the floor of their homes with elaborate black and white painted bowls placed over the heads of the deceased. Eight hundred years later, grave robbers routinely dug up Mimbres burial sites for bowls worth thousands of dollars on the black market. Despite stiff penalties and fines, pot-hunting and illegal excavation of Indian sites continue in the Gila and other Southwestern wilderness settings.[15]

In the 1980s, new backpacking ethics and strict regulations concerning the number of people and animals in a group helped to preserve the pristine values of wilderness. The demographic of backpacking couples and families who enjoyed Wilderness areas year round had given way to organized education groups who come primarily during summer months and practice low-impact camping.[16] These groups also cleaned up after themselves, following the ethic of leaving a place better than it was found. In the 1990s, students from Texas A&M University hiked the trail to White Water Baldy and scattered more than fifty fire rings at abandoned camp sites. It's just one good sign that wilderness continues to offer peace and healing for well-intentioned souls who practice the etiquette of "Leave No Trace." Their efforts help the land heal itself from the scars of thoughtless campers who "civilized" a site by building fire pits and lean-tos, stacking firewood, and letting horses paw the ground near trees. As author of The Land Ethic, Leopold would applaud the "Leave No Trace" admonition.

# Our Wolf
## Ethic Inheritance

Andrew Gulliford

Of all the scholarship on Leopold, not enough has been written about his hunting across the West, in Wisconsin, and even into Mexico during his famous canoe trip to lagoons now severely depleted by water impeded by Colorado River dams. I believe that Leopold's land ethic, and his conservation values, came from his constantly being outdoors and learning to see and think like a hunter just as Theodore Roosevelt did. The two men embody conservation. As Richard Rubin explains in this book, Leopold would become a professor of game management at the University of Wisconsin and would pioneer what is now wildlife management.

But where Roosevelt and Leopold dramatically differed was understanding the role of top tier predators. Leopold made the transition from conservationist to environmentalist. He is an absolutely critical historical figure in that philosophical evolution. *A Sand County Almanac* contains two essential principles: The Land Ethic, and the meaning of his essay "Thinking Like A Mountain" to understand the predator-prey relationship that Theodore Roosevelt did not grasp. TR called wolves and mountain lions "beasts of waste and desolation." Leopold knew better.

Leopold understood the need for wolves in wildlife ecosystems. Here in Colorado, after years of efforts, wolves have returned to our state as a vital part of The Land Ethic. Leopold would be proud and eager to assess the pending ecological changes. With 5.8 million people in Colorado and much outdoor use, the experiment of reintroducing wolves has only just begun. Wolf history is important. Though this is a book about New Mexico, Leopold would agree that wildlife know no political boundaries.

In Colorado we have twelve streams named Wolf Creek, yet we killed off all our wolves. The frontier officially ended in 1890 and the last vestiges of wilderness had to be cleansed of their large predators, especially the feared, gray timber wolves, which may once have numbered in the thousands in Colorado. Now Proposition 114 *The Restoration of Gray Wolves* brought back the carnivore by December 31, 2023 west of the Continental Divide. Controversy continues especially since a small wolf pack has been confirmed by Colorado Parks and Wildlife to be living in Moffat County. We will need to learn to live with wolves again and it will not be easy.

Arthur Carhart's book *The Last Stand of the Pack* describes in grim detail the struggle to pursue and kill the last Colorado wolves. *The Last Stand of the Pack* is now back in print published by the University Press of Colorado in a critical edition edited by Tom Wolf and me.[17] All Carhart's original words are there and we added new essays on the eco-possibilities of wolf re-introduction. Few Coloradans remember his book, but across the nation Carhart is known for what he did at Trappers Lake in Rio Blanco County—he advocated for wilderness, for leaving wild landscapes alone.

The White River Museum of the Rio Blanco Historical Society has its own wolf pelt. This wolf is up against a wall secure in an ornate oak and glass display case in the back room of the museum. He's probably one of the best preserved of all Colorado's historic wolves. The wolf's amber eyes stare straight ahead and its bared teeth almost emit a growl, but he's safe enough in the storage area among bear traps, a two-headed calf, a sarsaparilla bottling machine, and an ornate sheep wagon. George Wilber and Les Burns killed him on Oak Ridge. He was the last wolf to die on the White River Plateau.

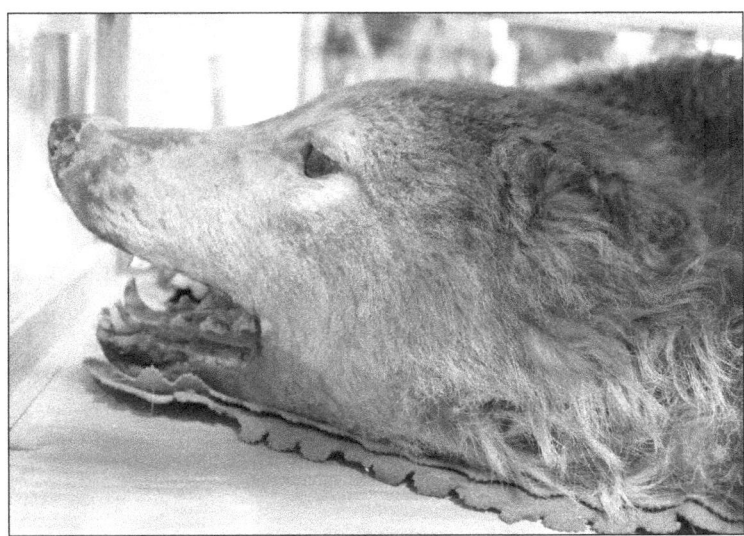

The wolf was shot in 1919. How ironic that in 1919, the same year Carhart had his vision about federal wilderness as an ideal, hunters killed the last wolf in Rio Blanco County. It took decades before Americans came to understand that wilderness without wildlife was just empty scenery.

The Bureau of Biological Survey claimed to have killed Colorado's last wolf in 1935. Scholar Michael Robinson believes the date was 1945 in Conejos County.[18] Either way it has been decades since Colorado's mountains have heard the full-throated howls of a wolf pack on a moonlit night, but that is changing. Wolf scat, photographs, and recorded howling have all confirmed a small pack of wolves in Moffat County. "Staff will continue monitoring the area as part of our overall wildlife management and conservation duties," explained former Colorado Parks and Wildlife director Dan Prenzlow.[19] As we learn to live with wolves, it is important to understand why we killed them off.

Wolves harassed livestock because wild game populations had dramatically dropped. Most of Colorado's elk had been shot and killed by market hunters who were paid ten cents a pound for elk, deer, and antelope. Today's elk herds evolved from elk transplanted from Montana and Wyoming and now Colorado has the largest elk population in North America. The state's elk herds are doing fine, but there are rising fears of chronic wasting disease. How to combat the disease? Introduce gray wolves to cull the weak, the young, and the sick. Wolves can help restore our Colorado ecosystems and ecosystems in New Mexico when they migrate south.

No one knows how wolves will fit into the Colorado landscape, but many of us are waiting to find out. If wolves arrive on their own, we'll have to live with where they appear. If wolves are introduced, there can be more flexibility on where they live and certainly more planning. Wolves will wear radio collars and if they harass livestock the animals can be located and retrieved.

Wolf reintroduction into Colorado will take time and patience. Folks who would never normally speak to each other, because they wear different hats, different footwear, drive different vehicles, and support different causes, will have to sit at the same table and share their values, their concerns, their hopes for their families, as well as their future. With 5.8 million people, Colorado is essentially an urban state with suburban sprawl on the Front Range and less than a quarter million people on the Western Slope where wolves will be introduced. We can adjust. We can learn to accommodate ourselves to another top tier predator besides ourselves. Certainly, farmers and ranchers have done so in Wisconsin, Michigan, Minnesota, Idaho, Montana, and Wyoming. But I admit, as a Colorado wildlife biologist told me, "More hearts have to be won."

Wolves are part of our Western wildlife heritage. Learning to live again with them in the Rocky Mountains may be one of our most important twenty-first century lessons in ecology and humility. We killed wolves with poisons, traps and guns. Arthur Carhart came to realize the pervasive power of industrialized death.

A year after publishing *The Last Stand of the Pack*, Carhart questioned co-author Stanley P. Young whether exterminating wolves "to please squawking stockmen" could be justified. "Isn't it a just consideration that the cats and wolves and coyotes have a damn sight better basic right to live in the hills and have use of that part of the world as their own than the domestic livestock of the stockmen?" he asserted.[20] Carhart, father of the wilderness idea, wanted wild creatures in wild places. So did Aldo Leopold.

"Wolves. We've progressed past them. We have too much industry and agriculture to ever go back to wolves," Dan Schwartz owner of Ripple Creek Hunting Lodge east of Meeker near Trappers Lake told me. "But they're coming. Wolves are here. You hear about them all the time. I don't think they'll decimate the elk population, but they'll change elk habitat. It'll be a completely different hunt. If they move down [from Yellowstone] the ecosystem will allow it, but to introduce them is insanity. We need to get ahead of the game on wolf management before the feds get involved."[21]

What would Carhart think of wolves returning to Colorado? As a wilderness advocate, a "wilderness prophet" in the words of author Tom Wolf, Carhart surely would have seen the connection between wild landscapes and *canis lupus*. As a hunter and a sportsman interested in healthy big game populations, he probably could have come to learn what Lewis and Clark understood and what Aldo Leopold tried to teach—that wolves have their place. I hunt wildlife and I agree—wolves belong. I am an elk hunter who welcomes the return of wolves to Colorado. Why would I want to compete for elk meat with another top tier predator? Some years I see no wild game and the only thing I cut up with my hunting knife is an orange.

Why would I willingly welcome more competition with elk numbers threatened by habitat fragmentation, disruption by mountain bikers, ATV riders, back country skiers, and hikers of all sorts? Folks move to Colorado and New Mexico for our outdoor opportunities. Climbers, hikers, bikers, and skiers are everywhere in the mountains at all times of the year. Elk, which are private animals preferring quiet meadows and south-facing winter hillsides, are constantly disturbed.

Why add wolves to the mix when there are already hunters galore seeking elk?

Because it is time for wolves. It is time for natural big game management. We spent the twentieth century manipulating nature. By 1910 commercial hunting had killed out all the elk in Colorado. We reintroduced them from Wyoming in 1916 with no legal elk hunting season until 1929. Now in the twenty-first century we need to restore an ecological balance. It is not easy to live with a top tier predator. Their ecological role in diverse ecosystems was not understood.

One of the nation's first ecologists, forester Aldo Leopold, shot a wolf from an Arizona rimrock and later regretted it. In his famous essay titled "Thinking like a Mountain" from *A Sand County Almanac* he wrote, "Only the mountain has lived long enough to listen objectively to the howl of a wolf…We reached the old wolf in time to watch a fierce green fire dying in her eyes. I realized then, and have known ever since, that there was something new to me in those eyes—something known only to her and to the mountain …

I thought that fewer wolves meant more deer, that no wolves would be a hunter's paradise."

He was wrong. Leopold lived long enough to change his views on predators and to become the first writer and proponent of game management, authoring an introductory textbook and teaching classes at the University of Wisconsin. Leopold scholar Susan Flader wrote, "The wolf, as one of the large carnivores, belonged at the very apex of the biotic pyramid…it became Leopold's symbol of the pyramid itself…of land health."[22] Leopold's ideas evolved.

As a hunter I value my time outdoors with friends, getting up before dawn, waiting for first light, trying to spot big game moving in the shadows and waiting for sunrise and a positive identification of the right species and the right sex. I prefer to hunt cow elk because of their flavorful meat, but I am not a trophy hunter. Hunting for me is being outside scanning, looking, using binoculars to scout ridges, and developing the patience it takes to wait all day, moving from location to location with my mind empty and my heart open for the gift of wild game. Do I want to share my hunts with wolves? Yes. I want a complete, intact ecosystem, part of Aldo Leopold's Land Ethic. Landscape is as important to me as big game. We have much to learn from wolves and we have failed to learn their eco-lessons. Wolves hunt sick and diseased animals. That is their ecosystem role and they make prey herds healthier.

"The eradication of wolves in Colorado was a moral, ethical, and ecological mistake. We owe functional ecosystems to future Coloradans, and wolves are an important part of those ecosystems," explains biologist Gary Skiba, Wildlife

Program Manager for San Juan Citizens Alliance. He adds, "The idea that wolves will harm prey populations is nonsense. Wolves and their prey evolved together for hundreds of thousands of years, including about 15,000 years in Colorado since the last ice age. The role of wolves in removing sick and injured prey has been demonstrated over and over."

Skiba notes, "Reintroduction of wolves is pretty simple, and we have plenty of experience to do it efficiently and effectively. Restoration can be done humanely and in a way that is respectful of the needs and concerns of all Coloradans."[23]

It is time to restore nature and to allow wolves to play their role in what Leopold called the centuries-old "evolutionary drama." Will wolves pursue the same elk I hunt? Possibly, but they'll also make me a better hunter, more wary, more cautious, more connected to the outdoors. Yes, this is a historic moment for our state and for the West. For the first time a state's citizens have required state officials to take an action three times denied by the State Wildlife Commission. Citizens have spoken. Colorado Parks and Wildlife needs to comply, but there should be plenty of time for dialogue, discussion, education, and hopefully consensus, including information on the illegality of poaching or killing introduced wolves.

We need to learn to live with *Canis lupus*. We need to hear their howls on moonlit nights deep in the Weminuche Wilderness or high on the Flattops Wilderness in Northwest Colorado. Gray shadows should leave paw prints in snow beneath dark trees. Maybe wolves will even return to their old haunts where Carhart wrote about them in Unaweep Canyon, on the Book Cliffs, along Huerfano Creek, beside the Purgatoire River. Wolf recovery in Colorado will be a grand experiment. I wish Arthur Carhart and Aldo Leopold were alive to write about it. They would love to record the cycle of ecological change and humans foregoing hubris for humility. *The Last Stand of the Pack* is a valuable historical account. Now in the twenty-first century, we will turn a new page and allow a top tier predator to restore balance to our high-altitude ecosystems.

# A New Mexico Homescape Land Ethic

## Richard Rubin

Leopold was often emphatic that the Land Ethic should be a private landowner's responsibility, as well as the government's. In "The Ecological Conscience" section of "The Land Ethic" essay he asserts:

> Conservation is a state of harmony between men and land. Despite nearly a century of propaganda, conservation still proceeds at a snail's pace; progress still consists largely of letterhead pieties and convention oratory. On the back forty we still slip two steps backward for each forward stride (op. cit., p. 196).

Then in the "Substitutes for a Land Ethic" section, he goes on:

> There is a clear tendency in American conservation to relegate to government all necessary jobs that private landowners fail to perform … . The answer, if there is any, seems to be in a land ethic, or some other force which assigns more obligation to the private landowner (op. cit., pp. 200–201).

While the Shack land had grown to 120 acres by the 1940s, I submit you do not need dozens or hundreds of acres to practice conservation. Leopold's reference to the proverbial "back forty" of a farm implies the most neglected section of a traditional homestead allotment. Our New Mexico home was built on a half-acre of depleted alfalfa field. But we have done much here in land ethic spirit that "Enlarges the boundaries of the community to include *soils, waters, plants, and animals* (op. cit., p. 192, my italics).

We apply the term *homescape* to combine the physical place with the culture we bring to it. A Googled definition reveals more: "a meaningful place that is familiar enough to call home but also exists within a living, breathing, changing environment and cultural landscape." Our consciousness is expanded as Ed Yong evokes in *An Immense World* (Random House, 2023):

> The majesty of nature is not restricted to canyons and mountains. It can be found in the wild of perception … . To perceive the world through

> other senses is to find splendor in familiarity, and sacred in the mundane (p. 353).

Our relationship to this land in the high plains below El Salto Peak and the Carson National Forest is similar to William deBuys's description in *River of Traps: A Village Life,* (University of New Mexico Press, 1990).

> There were people in the mountain landscape whom I could not ignore. They had used the land and ultimately altered it. Even more interesting was the question of how the land had altered them, how natural history had shaped the history of cultures (pp. 56–57).

Much of the information related here is selected from my book with spouse Annette *Homescape Rewilding: stories of ordinary ecological practices,* (Nighthawk Press, 2021). We began with ideas that informed our right attitudes, like the guidance by Paul Kingsnorth in his *Confessions of a Recovering Environmentalist and other essays,* (Greywolf Press, 2017):

> One: Withdrawing … . so that you can allow yourself to sit back quietly and feel, intuit, work out what is right for you, and what Nature might need from you … . Two: Preserving non-human life … . Three: Getting your hands dirty. Root oneself in the work of land and place … . Four: Insisting that nature has a value beyond utility … . Five: Building refuges … . preserve what is of value—creatures, skills, things, places (pp. 145–147).

We have avoided conventional lawns and landscaping in our relationship to the house's yard. Instead, we add ecology and culture values to the concept of home in the term homescape. In his introduction to a collection of essays *The Next West*, (Island Press 1997), Donald Snow quotes a September 1942 article Leopold published in *Audubon* magazine:

> To analyze the problem of action, ... grasp that government, no matter how good, can only do certain things. Government can't raise crops, maintain small, scattered structures...or bring to bear on small, local matters that combination of solicitude, foresight, and skill which we call husbandry ... .
> Husbandry is the heart of conservation.

That word husbandry may sound archaic and stilted, but I again go back to my 1966 *Random House Unabridged Dictionary*. I divulge fondness for this older source than current Wikipedia because this  tome was inherited from my scientist father. I also think this is the language Leopold would have known in his early twentieth century Lawrenceville Prep and Yale education. From the Old English, the archaic verb *to husband* meant to till, cultivate. In Middle English, the noun *husbandry* described farming and agriculture. In addition, I found a definition of careful, thrifty management or conservation. And another stating the management of domestic affairs or of resources generally. Hmm, conservation and management of resources. And per Leopold, a Land Ethic should guide both public and private action.

## Soils

Enlarging our community consciousness in Leopold's way, Annette and I have always enjoyed *petrichor*, the scent of rain on dry soil. It is especially distinct in the Southwest, particularly after summer monsoon rains. *Petra* refers to stone and one reference attributed *ichor* to Greek mythology, golden fluid that flows in the veins of the Olympian gods. The word's source is geochemistry, apparently coined by two Australian scientists in 1964. For this homescape essay, the attractive fragrance draws us into kinship with the soil.

We proceeded at home by following Leopold's advice in the *Almanac* "December" essay:

> Acts of creation are ordinarily reserved for gods and poets, but humbler folk may circumvent this restriction if they know how. To plant a pine, for example, one need to be neither god nor poet; one needs only own a shovel (op. cit., p. 76).

The builder of our house provided five trees on the front swale facing east: a piñon, a ponderosa, two scotch pines, and an aspen. Yet the center rear and the perimeters south, west, and north called for more. Joining the Native Plant Society of New Mexico, Taos Chapter, I learned about Professor Jack Carter's *Trees and Shrubs of New Mexico* (Mimbres Publishing, 2012). Leopold observed in "The Land Pyramid" section of "The Land Ethic:" *"that the native plants and animals kept the energy circuit open; others may or may not.* (Leopold's italics, op. cit., p. 205).

And in the closing sentence of his 1948 Foreword to the *Almanac:* "Perhaps such a shift of values can be achieved by reappraising things unnatural, tame, and confined in terms of things natural, wild, and free" (op. cit., p. xxiii).

Carter specifies that thirteen conifers are native to Taos County. Eureka! We received our shovel mission orders. The evergreen category *conifer* includes pines, junipers, firs, and spruces. In some ways, we were following Leopold's vision for the University of Wisconsin Arboretum and Wildlife Refuge, a "wild institution."

You can evaluate the tree list and follow our planting process in the *Homescape Rewilding* book. And to pursue community with soils, we recognized that trees needed augmentation in our predominant alkaline clay, especially conifers. Therefore, we added acidified cotton burr mulch on planting.

## Waters

For this phase of our Leopoldian homescape story, I offer an anecdote Meine relates from 1936:

> Aldo, Starker, and Luna had toyed around with the idea of "building a little forest for ourselves" on the [Shack] property. The two-year-old plantations at the university arboretum provided a personal precedent for Leopold. His trip to Germany sold him on the idea. He ordered a thousand white pines and a thousand red pines from a nursery in Madison. "Oh, Aldo," Estella said in surprise, "that's going to be so much work. You couldn't order less than that?" Aldo explained, "You have to get a certain minimum, or you can't get any at all." Aldo hired a neighbor farmer named Webster to plow some furrows in the sandy soil. In April, during the university's spring break, the family moved up to the shack and planted two thousand pine trees and dozens of shrubs—mountain ash, juneberry, nannyberry, cranberry, raspberry, plum. That spring was one of the driest on record … . Spring warmed into summer, and still no rain fell … . Leopold recorded the tree mortality figures: Norway pines 95% dead, Whites 99% dead, Mt. Ash 100% dead, Tamaracks 50% dead … . They would have to try again the following spring (pp. 364–365).

I include this story to show how we respected Leopold's attention to water among the Land Ethic components. This is particularly crucial in Northern New Mexico where we revere *Water is Life*. The earliest nomadic tribes traveled to follow seasonal water sources. Choice of place became more important as maize, bean, and squash crops were introduced, and group settlements developed. The next phase of traditional settlers, Puebloans, used various water capture methods. The seventeenth century Hispanic colonists brought the *acequia* system learned from the Moors. The word is from the Arabic *al-saqiya* meaning "irrigation ditch." The peak above us is named El Salto which means "The Falls" and the runoff surface water is organized into *acequias*. More than just irrigation, the system is a legal entity of water rights, community distribution, and cultural heritage recognized by the state of New Mexico.

But the imposition of United States law after the Mexican American War changed the control of land and water. Three *acequias*, including the *Madre* mother ditch, run from east to west through the section of land that became our neighborhood. But the rights to any water were sold off by the developer. Therefore, our homescape planting required us to create other water sources to avoid the tragedy of Leopold's trees. Our Land Ethic consciousness opened to thinking like trees in relation to water. But we did not just install plastic tubing and numerous emitters regulated by clocks attached to our house water supply as frequently done here. Our primary house supply is a well about one hundred feet deep into the underground river flowing off El Salto. Given variations in summer monsoon rains, snowpack, and drought cycles, this water source should not be blindly exploited.

## The Aridity Challenge at Mi Casita

Water was scarce in Tres Piedras where Leopold chose to situate Mi Casita in 1911. There are no continuous, reliable sources among the rocks. That is one reason no population settled there before the Denver and Rio Grande Railroad was built beginning in 1880. The Forest Service was ingenious in providing multiple sources for the new supervisor's home. From the 1991 Historic Registration documents, we can identify the water impoundment just south of the house. It is shallow, about a hundred feet in diameter, and connects to a cistern by a gravel filtration route. As a source of domestic water, the cistern is twenty-five feet deep and protected by a shack, still evident. There was also a stock pond east of the entry road, now replaced by a modern septic tank.

However, in my frequent walkabouts around the house, I found a likely original water system not recorded. About fifty feet uphill in the west rocks, a concrete cube is wedged. It is twelve feet on a side and railroad tie pieces support the roof which has a foot diameter hatch. A concrete slab is adjacent, and a two-inch pipe protrudes. Going towards the house, a crook of thick rebar extends out of a pipe underground. I conclude the cube collected runoff water that froze, and a holding tank on the slab fed house needs. There is also a slab above the barn that ranger consultants have figured once held a tank. This entire water system was replaced much later with a deep well one third mile west when a new ranger station was built and pipes extended down to Mi Casita.

## Our Homescape Water Conservation

Back at home, we added much absorbent humus to the soil. Then we mulched the trees and shrubs. Knowing that the trees, our vegetable beds, and corn *milpa* would require a great deal of continuous water, I had a roof catchment tank installed. This is 1700 gallons and is pressured by its own pump, run off electricity from our rooftop solar array. A manifold of valves allows connection of hoses leading to specific needs, such as one for the corn patch and one for spot watering the raised beds of tomatoes, cucumbers, and pumpkins, as well as peach and plum trees seasonally. Since much rain and snowmelt are not caught, we have six fifty-gallon barrels around the house under gutters and *canales* off the roof. People have asked if all that watering management seems like too much work, and our answer is that we are glad to have an active nurturing relationship with the homescape husbandry.

## Plants

This brings us to the third of Leopold's Land Ethic community entities. Beyond the extensive arboretum, now numbering seventy-five trees, and our victory garden horticulture, we encouraged a profusion of native shrubs, grasses, and forbs. A traditional *latilla* aspen pole fence encloses the rear one third acre, serving several purposes of windbreak, bird perching sites, intrusive prairie dog and western cottontail exclusion, family dog containment, and aesthetic addition to our view to the west. Along the inside, the native plant diversity includes blue spruce, bristlecone pine, Apache plume, mountain mahogany, Maximilian sunflowers, chokecherry, red osier dogwood, three leaf sumac, golden currant, and fernbush. Then towards the center, we added showy milkweed, purple cone flowers, blue flax, mock orange, Rocky Mountain penstemon, coral honeysuckle, bee balm, and more than that. What grows now is usually self-seeded. Then inside further, we planted a mix of native prairie grasses that we do not mow. Little creatures like the cover of stems year-round. Last, along the patio wall, Woods rose with creeping mahonia on the surface enjoy the roof runoff. On the several feet of slope down from the house, a rock garden contains a few dozen native flowers that are constantly changing. Yes, we encourage wildness and serendipity.

## Animals

A great value of these trees and native plants is the creation of habitat for more than human life. All year round, we love our bird companions. Here's an op-ed piece I wrote for the *Taos News*, published March 2, 2023:

> ### In Community with Doves
>
> For several years, a pair of doves has made our Arroyo Seco home habitat their own. Annette and I greatly appreciate their relationship with us, so I am moved to explore deeper understanding. As an old doctor, I also like sharing a prescription to enhance life in Taos. The idea of humans in community with all life, including the land, has become more important for environmental health. Beginning with experiences as a young forester in Arizona and New Mexico,

Aldo Leopold's practices evolved to recognize that "we abuse land because we regard it as a commodity belonging to us; when we see land as a community to which we belong, we may begin to share it with love and respect." Two methods directed his actions and teaching: first, advancing the science of Ecology which is devoted to studying the relationships among living things; and second, applying the practice of Phenology to observe and record the timing of seasonal events in nature, including phenomena such as seed dispersal, plants blooming, wildlife movements, birds nesting, and weather changes. These attitudes require profound attention to our environment, inspired traditionally in New Mexico by Native values and Norteno *querencia*. And I add influence from Frank Waters' writings and his contribution establishing the first conservation easement in the Taos Land Trust.

While Annette and I have dozens of bird species living in and passing through our Arroyo Seco homescape, why are these doves so engaging of our attention? First, they appear almost always together, having mated for life. Even when not perched together on the *latilla* fence, one is not far from the other. Their size and light coloring are eye catching. They tend to fly low in our visual range, often feeding on the ground in our garden patches. They also display themselves in regular ways, such as catching the morning sun perched on our *milpa* entrance pergola. The historic human tradition of naming, as recorded in the Bible's creation story, sends me to the dictionaries. Professor Ruben Cobos translates *palomita* as turtledove. This is a European species whose qualities have been applied to a gentle, loving person. Biblical symbolism for two turtledoves represents the Old and New Testaments. That is their meaning in the Christmas song. A village in Southern New Mexico was named *Las Palomas* after the nearby remedial natural springs. Many cultures have assigned special ceremonies to the birds, often for protection or peace. These range among worldwide Indigenous tribes, ancient Hebrews in the Noah's flood story, Aphrodite in Greek mythology, in Islam helping Mohammed, and in the baptism of Jesus. Modern practices include release at Olympic games and Papal coronations. And we remember the iconic Woodstock poster, perched on the guitar handle.

Our home companions are native Mourning doves, *Zenaida macroura*. The name has been assigned from their haunting, sad song. The word dove derives from Old English and Norse languages. While they breed for life, ornithologists have not identified mourning behavior at a partner loss, but now scholars are appreciating more the complex emotional life of other creatures. When our house was finished in 1993, I planted two ponderosa pines on the west side. These trees are now forty feet tall and thirty feet wide. The doves use both for their brood nests, usually two a year. I can tell the favorite locations from guano collections below. In Spring, we see the male alone collecting materials for his mate's nest building. They are said to be great parents, sharing the egg incubation and production of food for chicks from their digestive crops. Later, fledglings add more guano, and eventually each squab appears out, perching around our yard with the parents. Various seeds are their only food, so we are happy to keep the feeders filled year-round, as well as planting sunflowers and sharing our *milpa* corn. Ornithologists say they are very intelligent as well as loving and peaceful. These birds must have hardy and resilient qualities also, as they persist living here despite our recent wildfires and climate changes. That seems to say we are sharing healthy community relationships.

There are many more avian residents and visitors to our homescape. From crows and magpies, to flickers and downy woodpeckers, pinyon and scrub jays, robins, grossbeaks, and towhees, sparrows and wrens, winter chickadees and more I can't identify; we are delighted by the vitality. It helps that I maintain year-round seed feeders and a winter suet station. We appreciate the thrills of hummingbirds entertaining us from April to September. And yes, there are some top of the pyramid predators such as red tail hawks and we occasionally find barn owl prey remnants.

I am glad people are recognizing the value of insects in ecological consciousness. Sure, attracting pollinators is popular. In addition, native bees live in the *latilla* fence posts cut from aspen. Rodents can be good, too. Don't overlook the garden bacteria, fungi, nematodes, and worms. We maintain a ranch of red wigglers for summer composting. And to maintain normal habitat for the multitude of nocturnal creatures, we remove the solar path lights among the garden beds during the nesting and blooming seasons.

Finally, our domestic companions can expand appreciation of the biotic community. Like Leopold's sojourns with his spaniel Flick, I learn from my German water retriever sidekick Troi. Leopold wrote in the July *Almanac* essay:

> We sally forth the dog and I, at random. He has paid scant respect to all those vocal goings-on [bird songs], for to him the evidence of tenantry is not song, but scent. Any illiterate bundle of feathers, he says, can make a noise in a tree. Now he is going to translate for me the olfactory poems that who-knows-what silent creatures have written in the summer night (op. cit., p 41).

# Our Taos Community
## National Monument
### Richard Rubin

Since Leopold's day, the categories of public lands have grown substantially. As the U.S. Forest Service evolved from the Forest Reserves of the Department of Agriculture in 1905, so did the Bureau of Land Management from the nineteenth century General Land Office under the Interior Department. The National Park Service was created by presidential order in 1916 to manage the existing entities since the 1872 establishment of Yellowstone. The designated parks have now grown to four hundred nationally. The formation of new wilderness areas crossed agency lines between the Agriculture and Interior Departments. New designations of Wilderness Study Areas and National Conservation Lands were added.

The Antiquities Act of 1906 gave the president authority to proclaim National Monuments on lands already under federal jurisdiction. These are defined by the Bureau of Land Management as an area of land and water that is afforded protection because of historic and scientific interest.

Since 1906, 161 have been created by presidents and 40 by Congress. In Land Ethic evolution spirit, the recognition of these monuments has evolved. Of these 201, 129 continue and 72 were "redesigned" into entities such as national parks, national preserves, national forests, wildlife refuges, and one returned to a Native American tribe.

According to the Bureau of Land Management website (BLM.gov), the National Landscape Conservation System was established in 2010 for public lands to ensure conservation protection, manage entities as part of the larger landscape, raise awareness of the value of the landscape conservation system, and build on the BLM's commitment to conservation. This program is authorized by Congress until 2025. However, we have a more recent piece of legislation influencing our conservation interests. The John Dingell Conservation Management and Recreation Act of 2019 consolidates federal and state lands to protect recreation opportunities and provide access, again according to the BLM information website.

In the Foreword to a beautiful photography book *Our National Monuments: America's Hidden Gems* by QT Luong,[33] Sally Jewell wrote:

> As a childhood immigrant to the United States, my family developed a deep appreciation of nature through exploring the towering forests and dazzling waters of our new home in the Pacific Northwest. In the six-plus decades since, I have witnessed population growth and development alter these landscapes, making it clear that without sensible protections, everything is vulnerable.

## OUR TAOS COMMUNITY NATIONAL MONUMENT

> In serving as US Secretary of the Interior under President Barack Obama, I came to further understand the irreplaceable value and uniqueness of America's public lands and waters and the importance of listening to the collective knowledge of the original stewards of these natural gifts—indigenous communities whose ancestors lived in harmony with nature for thousands of years. With each passing year, modern science blends with traditional knowledge to evolve our understanding of what is needed to shape a sustainable future for all life on land and sea…
>
> Humanity is awakening to the importance of intact lands, waters, and ecosystems to our health and well-being, and the stresses we have placed on them through our actions. Before settlement by newcomers, American public lands were shared common resources of indigenous communities who understand the importance of taking only what was needed. With the protections chronicled in this book, and others being studied and advocated for by a wide variety of citizens, I am hopeful our grandchildren and the generations to follow will be thankful that these lands and waters were protected, and their curiosity nurtured by a deeper understanding of nature's capacity to provide all living beings with a sustainable future (p. 8).

So how can we find our way to Land Ethic community consciousness and practices among this culture, agency, and regulation complexity? A thorough discussion would require a journalistic career or doctoral thesis. Here's a recent small story of my odyssey attempting to do an ecological good deed in the junction of private and public lands. This is an early version of my article later published in the *Taos News*, October 19, 2023.

### A Wild Skunk Conundrum

A common striped skunk *Mephitis mephitis* raided my northern New Mexico corn patch and provoked a conundrum of humane ecology, homestead rights, and public land regulations. Sorting this out to a happy conclusion for all concerned proved adventurous. My initial intervention of coyote urine crystals from the hardware store failed to repel continued nocturnal raids. A gardener friend advised mothballs to hang in bags on the fence. Nope, no effect. An experienced farmer neighbor said get a Havahart live trap. Well, it worked, but now I had the dilemma of proper return to the wild. This prompted a call to Taos County Animal Control for disposal advice. I wanted release somewhere back in the ecosystem, not killing. The agent said they don't handle skunks and gave me two options: a private critter control outfit or drop it off myself somewhere in the mountains. And oh yes, cover the trap when you approach with a tarp to minimize alarming it and block possible spray.

Not wanting to leave him in the yard and risk spraying my dogs through the trap, an agile friend and I carried the cage about four hundred yards into a large fallow conservation easement field. However, he was back the next night, confirming that skunks range widely, especially males. The Havahart company website advises release at least ten miles away. As I'm bandying this story around, I hear that it's popular to dump skunks on public land west of me, across the Rio Grande Gorge, colloquially *otra banda,* the other side.

I belong to a Facebook Taos Farm and Garden group. We trade home garden queries, show off harvests, inquire for help with problems, etc. My posting of the "across the gorge" idea received surprising hostility from a few people living there about dumping it in their yards, even though the potential territory is very large. A few people said, "Just shoot it." I also got accusations of animal cruelty taking the creature away from his family and home range. The *otra banda* area in question has a few rugged individualist and counter cultural settlements.

Therefore, I started thinking about appropriate public lands for release since much "over there" is Bureau of Land Management domain, including a large designated National Conservation Area for wildlife. I called the Taos BLM office for approval. The clerk commiserated with my garden losses, said they have no policy on this issue, and directed me to the New Mexico Department of Game and

Fish. The main office in Santa Fe verified that this trapping was legal on my own property, so a license was not required. She gave me the phone numbers of the local Taos game wardens. These two guys both responded similarly, saying that there are no regulations for skunks as "non-game animals." They said to take it ten miles away onto public lands because the BLM and the US Forest Service have no restrictions on freeing trapped skunks. So wrapping the cage in a tarp, this guy rode in my pickup bed, with my care to drive smoothly. I set the trap down in the BLM National Conservation Area, gave him time to calm, then opened the door. He took off at a fast waddle across the sage field.

In caution though, as skunks are often seen around my neighborhood traveling the road and *acequias* at night, I set the trap again. This time I learned that skunks have competitors for fragrant sardine bait. I caught a handsome tabby housecat without a collar. He was released nearby to return home or take his chances in feral life. A week later, no more corn ears have been chewed, so now we are enjoying some ourselves.

And my practices for relationship with the more-than-human-world have evolved through this experience. Swapping this homescape yarn with my longtime plumber, he related dealing with a skunk family under his mother's house south of town in

Ranchos de Taos. He borrowed a trap from the county agriculture extension agent and first used cat food as bait. But he ended up catching neighborhood felines. He switched to fresh eggshells and succeeded with the skunk family, one at a time. So I gave the eggshell method a try, acquired another *mephitis* cousin, and took another ride to the BLM land *otra banda.* Our trap now sits in the corn patch, unbaited but ready just in case. Que sera, sera up here in the foothills.

## Our Nearby Monument

Land Ethic experience need not be abstract or distant. The Rio Grande del Norte National Monument is a 242,555-acre area of public lands in Taos County, New Mexico. It was proclaimed as a National Monument on March 25, 2013 by President Barack Obama under the provisions of the Antiquities Act. The monument includes two BLM recreation areas, a portion of the Rio Grande designated as a Wild and Scenic River, and the Wild and Scenic Red River section. On March 12, 2019, the John Dingell, Jr. Conservation, Management, and Recreation Act designated two federal wilderness areas within the Monument: the Rio San Antonio Wilderness in the northwest corner, and the Cerro del Yuta Wilderness in the northeast corner. From the BLM Website:

The Rio Grande del Norte National Monument is comprised of rugged, wide-open plains at an average elevation of 7,000 feet, dotted by volcanic cones, and cut by steep canyons with rivers tucked away in their depths. The Rio Grande carves an 800-foot-deep gorge through layers of volcanic basalt flows and ash. Among the volcanic cones in the Monument, Ute Mountain is the highest, reaching 10,093 feet.

This area has attracted human activity since prehistoric times. Evidence of ancient use is found throughout the area in the form of petroglyphs, prehistoric dwellings, and many other types of archaeological sites. More recent activity includes abandoned homesteads from the 1930s.

The monument is an important area for wintering animals and provides a corridor by which wildlife move between two mountain ranges.

The unique setting of the Monument also provides a wealth of recreational opportunities. Whitewater rafting, hunting, fishing, hiking, mountain biking, and camping are some of the more outstanding activities that can be enjoyed in the Monument.

## OUR TAOS COMMUNITY NATIONAL MONUMENT

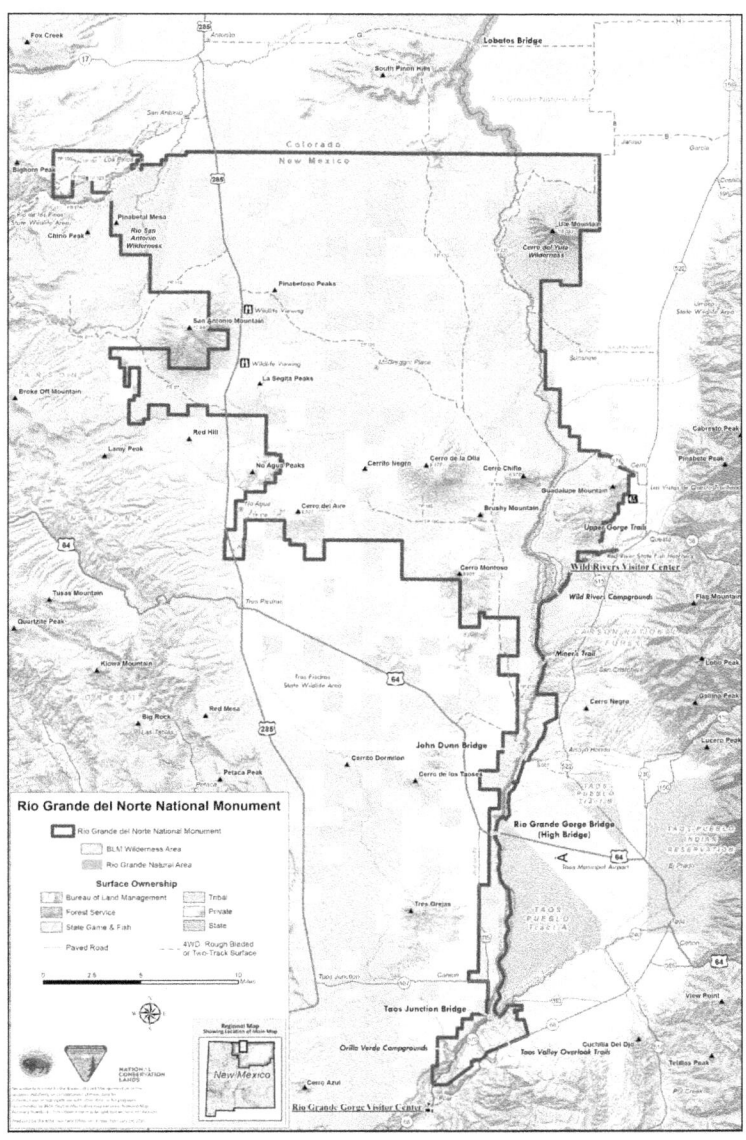

MAP COURTESY BUREAU OF LAND MANAGEMENT WEBSITE.

The Rio Grande del Norte National Monument and Wild Rivers Visitor Center is located in Cerro, NM at 1120 Cerro Road. Go north from Questa on NM 522 and turn left on State Road 378; the Visitor Center is about 17 miles from the turnoff.

Here's an example of a Land Ethic experience for kids there. Tim Long has been the BLM Ranger host at the Visitor Center for over a decade. We are acquainted as he taught music to our son Dan at Hummingbird Camp in Jemez Springs thirty years ago. When Dan and family visited here from their Philadelphia home last summer, we took a trip to the Monument. Tim led seven-year-old Spencer through the Junior Ranger educational initiation and awarded him a badge that he happily wore home.

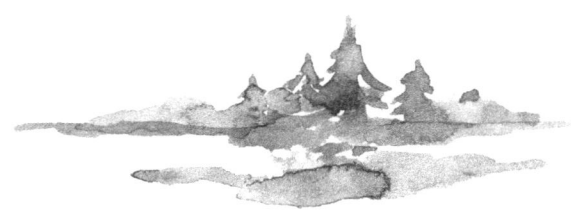

The Rivers & Birds Program, based in Arroyo Seco, New Mexico, has provided opportunities for many Taos area school children to know the Land Ethic. Founder Roberta Salazar served seventeen years as a federal government wildlife biologist and began this education program twenty-three years ago. Its mission:

> To advocate for conservation of our public lands and provide experiential environmental education that celebrates the interconnection of all life, inspiring individuals to be leaders for Earth stewardship and peace (www.riversandbirds.org).

The Friends of Mi Casita sponsored an R&B group on a Mi Casita visit and teaching tour in 2023, including avian residents from the Santa Fe Raptor Center. One of the Rivers & Birds programs is "Kids in the Monument" where students celebrate and explore the Rio Grande del Norte Monument and practice conservation ethics.

Roberta wrote the Rio Grande del Norte National Monument description in QT Luong's survey book. I quote the final paragraph:

> Our local community (including Taos Pueblo, Hispanic land-based organizations, ranchers, local governments, businesses, and environmentalists) recognizing the extraordinary natural and cultural heritage of this place, worked together to request this landscape be permanently protected for the benefit of present and future generations. Today, Rio Grande del Norte National Monument is a tribute to the resilience and determination of a culturally diverse community that has survived and thrived for centuries in a sometimes harsh but always beautiful land (op.cit., p. 252).

Counted among today's deeply insightful New Mexico teachers of ecology, I asked Roberta for her view of Aldo Leopold's influence and value that continues from the source at Mi Casita:

Aldo Leopold embraced the interconnected nature of Earth's community and how it provides endless fascinating learning experience. His appreciation was not just for the amazing ecological niches of species but of the dynamic interplay within the whole.

Great learning should be full of wonder and exploration. Leopold expressed the importance of recreation in nature. We recreate our significance as part of the wild nature of this planet when we immerse ourselves in the outdoors.

Aldo Leopold loved Northern New Mexico and built a house for his family there which he named Mi Casita. Decades later, local environmental education organizations like Rivers and Birds are still following his lead, taking thousands of elementary school students into Nature on our federal public lands. The children are inspired to playfully realize the beautiful and profound interconnection of Nature and their place as caretakers in it.

This intergenerational approach mingles wise elders with energetic inquisitive youth just like the forests around them—where the grandmother trees anchor the younger trees as they grow into their special place in the forest.[34]

# Exploring
## Querencia as a Land Ethic
Leeanna Torres

**When the relationship between people and land are intertwined…**

> *I come from a land-based culture—tierra y agua—and what this means is my cultura has engrained in me the value attached to place attached to resources attached to life. In essence then, New Mexico's people and landscape, is querencia: "…That which gives a sense of place, that which anchors us to the land…a deeply rooted knowledge of place…"*
> — JUAN ESTEVAN ARELLANO [35]

The Hispanic Land Grants of New Mexico were granted within them "all the resources needed to sustain a community." The Tomé Land grant boundaries once included:

— To the East, the Manzano mountains.

— To the West, the Rio Grande River Valley, a wild and ephemeral river prone to flooding (and nutrient-heavy) before it was dammed in the early 1970s.

— To the South, land along the river for people to build houses and raise families.

— To the North, more land flanked by river and mountain, lumber and rock, soil and water, sun and sky.

Within the boundaries of Tomé's *merced* (favored grant) was forest land for lumber and hunting; *llano* (grasslands) for common-land grazing, farmland set upon a riparian corridor which received water from the Rio Grande River by means of spring flooding and *acequia* (irrigation ditch) systems. In essence, the community of Tomé held and maintained within it all it needed to *gift* the community sustainment thru its soil, water, grazing lands, and mountains. And this is how many of the Hispanic land grants around Nuevo Mexico were established and maintained—*communidad*. Was this a formal land ethic stated in science or policy? No, it was written in the history and sustenance of its people, and those of us blessed to inherit upkeep of *la merced* were also given great responsibility. Though in his seventies now, my Papa describes gathering cattle and sheep from the common grazing-lands of *la merced* at the foot of the Manzano Mountains. This place was his *querencia*—the place of work, responsibility, but also the place and space that shaped him as a young boy. My father grew up in both farm and ranch even after *la merced* was lost to greed and conflict, and he continues to pass his *querencia* on to his children and grandchildren, one of whom is me.

Widely known authors such as J. Drew Lanham might refer to *querencia* as "home-place"; similarly, Robin Wall Kimmerer might call it "kinship." But here in Nuevo Mexico this "interconnectedness" is more commonly referred to as "*querencia*." With its roots in the Spanish verb *querer*—"to want, to love"—the term *querencia* continues to reveal itself in my own journey as a native daughter of New Mexico.

Aldo Leopold taught that "the Land Ethic simply enlarges the boundaries of the community to include soils, waters, plants, and animals, or collectively: the land." (*A Sand County Almanac*, op. cit., p. 192.)

### *Tierra* (Soil)

A few days before his last breath, *Tío* Eppy begged his brother (my father), to take him outside, insisting he needed to see the corrals, the cattle, the farm fields. So with the help of his two sons and youngest brother, *Tío* Eppy was helped up from the bed, and taken out just across the road to the place of his *querencia*. Flanked by the old work shed (crowded with tools and tractor parts), *Tío* Eppy looked out into the alfalfa fields given to him by his own father. An inheritance. And then reaching down, slow and with wracking pain throughout his body, *Tio* Eppy grabbed a fist-full of dirt in both hands. Both fists trembled, shook, an unspoken and unnamed urgency, and he gripped the *tierra* between palms and fingers, nails and fingertips, his hands tense and tight on the very earth itself. Was he preparing to leave? Was he speaking back to the land in an unnamed desperation? Was he afraid, and thus clinging to that which he knew most intimately, the earth itself? Or was it much more? And am I allowed to even mention a moment so intimate?

*Tio* Eppy knew he was dying—we all knew he was dying—and yet all he wanted to do was grip dirt. His hands held the *tierra*, and the three men stood there in silence for what was a long time, in the shade of the *alamo* (cottonwood tree).

*Querencia* for a place is more than just strength, more than just endurance. And so too, the idea of land health, land ethic, is more than just ethic. It is a true thing, like the soil between the fingers of a dying man.

## *Agua* (Water)

When I was a child, Papa taught me how to drink water from the outside hose, a faded green garden hose coiled neatly on the concrete pad against his work shed. On summer afternoons, when the heat was at its peak and our thirst was greatest, he taught me and my brother how to turn on the water first, then let it run a bit, because the water would come out scalding hot. In this very small lesson, he was sure to point out that we were to save this hot water, let it run into the adjacent bucket instead of spilling onto the concrete.

Papa taught us to save the water in the bucket for the birds and the dogs to drink. After a few seconds of running, the water would turn cool, coming up and out from the ground through the garden hose, and my *hermanito* (little brother) and I would drink from it, swallow that cold clean water, letting the remains fall into the bucket below, captured and never wasted.

When we recognize water as truly sacred, rather than biological, economical, or even political, how does this transform our actions and perspectives? And how do we reclaim water's beauty, blessings, and *querencia* even in the face/space of *politica*, pandemic, and mega-drought conditions?

*Mi familia, mi gente* did not tell me that water is sacred; instead, they showed me. Like water sprinkled on us during Día de San Juan. Like respect for the *acequia* that irrigates our fields. Like Nana pouring a bit of holy water from Easter's Mass into her beans on the stove.

The late Estévan Arellano was a gifted Hispano writer and activist who provided his definition:

> Querencia is that which gives us a sense of place, that which anchors us to the land, that which makes us a unique people, for it implies a deeply rooted knowledge of place, and for that reason we respect our place, for it is our home, and we don't want to violate our home in any way … . Our philosophy is borrowed from our Native American brothers, for we are brothers and sisters.[35]

*Agua* in our *cultura* is more than just metaphor, more than an economic commodity, more than a liquid bottled in plastic and purchased so cheaply at the Dollar Store or Walmart. Even graffiti art hidden beneath a city bridge speaks that our intrinsic knowing running in our blood and bones understands its spray-painted message—*Agua es vida.*

### *Rábanos*—Radishes (Plants)

Mama makes radish enchiladas on Tuesday afternoon. Walking into the kitchen, the familiar smell of "fresh" made tortillas greets me, along with red-chile in a slow September simmer. Television on in the background plays Mama's usual daily episode of "Judge Judy."

"What's the case about today?" I ask.

"Eeee, there's a lady that's after her landlord *por que* he tried kicking her out of the apartment!" replies Mama, her apron spattered with specks of white flour and smelling of fresh-cut onion.

As Judge Judy plays on, I move through Mama's kitchen, knowing since childhood where every kitchen tool and plate belongs. I begin grating cheese, while Mama starts dipping the tortillas in the chile, beginning to roll what will become tonight's enchilada dinner.

"Why did Abuelita make radish enchiladas?" I ask Mama, expecting her to explain it as Indigenous or cultural tradition.

Mama stops and thinks, her hands suddenly still, and she pauses for longer than I expect. She is thinking, and a commercial for Keller & Keller plays on in the background, their law office claiming in a confident masculine voice to "get you the money YOU deserve…"

Still looking to Mama, I'm surprised at her unexpected pause, and then circle back to my own question, surprised I'd never asked it before—Why did Abuelita make radish enchiladas?

Finally, Mama has an answer, and her hands return to her bowl and its spoon as she speaks, "*Saves que?* I think she did it only because they were so poor…*pienso que* they couldn't afford meat, and she just never had enough money for *carnita*, so Abuelita could only use the food she could grow in her own back yard, in her *jardin*…"

Since I was a child, Mama's made—only on special occasions—radish enchiladas. Chopped up radish into petite and perfect squares, along with yellow onion similarly diced, then using fresh, hand-made flour tortillas, dip them into red chile then roll—like thick cigars—assorted tight against each other like stacked soldiers, and bake after sprinkling some cheese, in the oven for about 10 to 15 minutes. Mama would make these enchiladas for my birthday, or when my Tios came over, or just on other holiday occasions. I'd never seen these type of enchiladas anywhere else, not in restaurants, or magazines. And while they were a part of my life growing up, I'd only known my Abuelita made them, but nothing more.

Judge Judy's demanding tone on the TV in the background fades as Mama's reply repeats again in my head, her hands taking a tortilla from the stack beside her, rolling an enchilada as easy as a song: "…they couldn't afford meat, so Abuelita used the food she could grow in her *jardin*…"

At Mama's answer, I realize I too often overlook the *pobreza* (poverty) experienced by my ancestors. On my Mama's side, they were just plain poor, no other way to say it. "I always remember my Abuelita having the biggest most beautiful garden…" explains Mama, and I lean into this thought as Mama begins arranging a tortilla with chopped *cebolla, rabanos,* and *queso.*

Imagining my Abuelita's backyard garden, I envision a small patch of earth, a young widow with five young children to raise. But even in this imagining, I am reminded that the origins of my Abuelita's garden—her *jardin*—originated out of poverty—*pobreza.* It is the stark reality I cannot ignore or forget, even distanced by time and generations. Abuelita's granddaughter—my mother—earned a master's degree in education and worked until she retired with a good pension. But along with this, Mama passed along the tradition of radish enchiladas born from a garden of *pobreza.* And it is my privilege now to enjoy these enchiladas as a tradition. It is this transformation of adaptability into a form of *querencia* that shapes us, moves us beyond sentimentality into an ethic of attention and connection that both feeds us and shapes us.

"Case for the defendant!" shouts Judge Judy from the living room television screen, but Mama and I pay no attention. We are rolling radish enchiladas—*juntas*—together.

Radishes are *rábanos*. Poverty is *pobreza*. But what of the translation between Abuelita's garden into Mama's kitchen, generations later, a span of struggle and love that cannot be put into words, but rather, is found only in the taste, the tradition.

Mama's flour tortillas are soft in my hands, and as my fingers grasp for the radish cubes in Mama's blue ceramic bowl, I imagine Abuelita there with us, looking up occasionally to watch Judge Judy too, the spirit of her *jardin* still ever-present in our ordinary lives.

*Querencia* is a deeply rooted love of place and people.

### *Coyoté* (Animals)

While taking Santiago to school one morning, our ATV kicking up dirt alongside the *acequia*, we notice suddenly an object. I slow down, and as we near, we see the carcass.

"What is *that* Mama?!", asks my boy, curious and unafraid, even as he sees the carcass for himself.

A dead coyote. We stop. I let him see the animal for himself—all fur and limbs. There is no blood or signs of trauma. Instead, the animal just lay dead, its mouth open askew. Santiago names him simply "Coyoté."

After dropping off my boy at school, I stop to drag the Coyoté carcass off the path and into the brush between the *acequia* and row of Siberian elm trees. Later that afternoon, on our way from school back home, Santiago quickly asks, *where's* Coyoté? as we drive by, and I show him, the carcass still visible as we pass on our way home.

Days pass, the stench of decay grows stronger. Then it fades. Coyoté's body deflates further and further into the soil and debris, then autumn leaves from the surrounding trees soon cover Coyote's corpse like snow. Coyoté's scientific name, *Canis latrans,* means "barking dog" in Latin.

"Mama, we're almost gonna pass Coyoté," Santiago reminds me on our mornings to school, remembering his resting place alongside the narrow road between *acequia* and *terreno*. "How did Coyoté die?" my boy asks, again and again, and I reply honestly, "*no se, mi hitio,* sometimes animals just die…all living things die."

My boy does not respond to this explanation, instead, he's quiet, as if fully accepting my words as truth. And we both sit in the wordless rumble of the ATV beneath us arriving at the school along the path of the ditch-bank.

The school year progresses, COVID masks come off, and my little boy is at last able to "see" his teacher and his classmates without the hidden protection he's been wearing since his first day of kindergarten. Days, then weeks go by. Each morning and afternoon, we pass Coyoté. Still dead, always dead, but we leave him be, his body now becoming only hair and bones, a meat-less shape. With alfalfa fields now dormant, and December quickly approaching, I'm glad winter is coming, to mask coyote's decomposition from my little boy, to make the carcass less noticeable. This is how Santiago learns about death. Daily, on our ride to school along the path the *acequia* outlines for us, always between alfalfa-field and *acequia*, and I hide nothing from him. I let him see. He looks. Always and often my boy remembers Coyoté, and we acknowledge his presence as we pass along the narrow dirt road. This is how Santiago learns about death.

"Hi Coyoté!" he says aloud, sometimes with a small wave as we pass. It is hardly ever joyful, instead, simply an acknowledgment.

Little do I realize, only a few months from now, as winter quickly becomes summer, nineteen children and two teachers will be killed in a shooting at an elementary school in Uvalde, Texas. This is how I learn about death. A deeper learning.

We ride on along the *acequia* road, dirt beneath our bike tires, only a bit of summer left before school starts again for my boy. Santiago sees and learns from Coyoté's decay beside the *acequia* on our way to school each day. A soft learning about the reality of death. As summer wanes, Coyote's decay reminds me of the violence Santiago has yet to witness or understand. I think about the mothers in Texas, the shape of their sorrow.

From now, until the end of time, I will be Santiago's mother. But more specifically, his *Mama.* Will he remember that I kept my jewelry in a cigar box? Will he remember that I loved classic country drinking songs and held a fondness for any *gavilan* (bird of prey)? What will he remember? But more importantly, what will I teach him? Pass on? He's only six years old, but often I wonder *how many more mistakes will I make in raising him?*

Life and living, death and dying—I think of these things as Santiago pedals his bicycle along the dirt path between house and school, that outlined path created by the *acequia* near our house. I'm pedaling too. *Acequias* have been a part of my life since birth—growing up a farmer's daughter, I was raised learning from Papa's practice of irrigating his fields in summertime. As I still remain within the Middle Rio Grande Valley, I often think about my own boy's relationship to *acequias*. What will he learn? How will I teach him? What influence will these waterways have on his upbringing, his identity? If he does not take on the vocation of farmer or rancher, how will *acequias* still inform his learning?

We cannot give *querencia*, instead, we can only offer and reveal our own, not hoping we will pass it on to the next generation, but rather, live with a confident insistence it will be passed on.

Watching him pedal on his bike, I see my boy's little sneakers, fast and strong on the black pedals of an orange bike. Together we ride on along the *acequia* road, dirt beneath our bike tires. "*Orale* Coyoté!" is my enthusiastic greeting as we pass the place that marks our remembrance, and Santiago lifts his hand to wave, a genuineness that makes me smile.

## Communidad

How does a community experience, as well as expand, the querencia ethic?

Recently, I've been following the monthly newsletter of chef Johnny Ortiz-Conchas from Taos.[36] In one of his written *recuerdos* (rememberings), he mentions that he's developing "an ecosystem of practices that reflect the terrain and culture we come from in New Mexico … . " This statement struck such a chord of truth in me when I read it, and it sparked in me glimpses of daily life I've taken for granted as ordinary, as they continue to shape me.

*Recuerdos* like Mama revealing "Oh I LOVE getting hugs from Del!" when his name comes up in a kitchen conversation. Del, a warm and generous soul from Tomé, whose hugs seem to embrace you with his soul, oddly tight at first, then holding so that it catches you by surprise. It is a surprise because he holds you in a deep embrace, a kind of hug only reserved for someone like a mother, but he shares these kinds of embraces often, among community members, with Mama and me, and it makes us feel loved.

*Recuerdos* like sitting through Mrs. Moya's afternoon *velorio* (prayer vigil), all of us masked due to COVID-19 and sparsely scattered, and we recited the rosary prayers behind bits of cloth that kept our mouths exposed, and yet still the place was full of prayer. At the same time, beauty and truth like my brother who names his *toro* (bull) "*Corazon*" (heart). The animal is large and black, like one you'd see in a western movie, all muscle and meat, thick black hide stark against the dusty backdrop of the family rancho at the foothills of the *Manzanos*.

*Recuerdos,* like the smell of alfalfa in summer, remembering those endless days when we used to play tag on the *pilas* (piles), a wild gathering of *primos* (cousins) playing, early afternoon or in the middle of the hot day, it never mattered, we always played. And it was wild and careless play, often resulting in cuts and scrapes and rash. Or opening up a box of Hostess Cakes or Little Debbie Cakes, remembering how Nana always had stacks of boxes in her kitchen cabinet, but it was Papa who made me love them. His affinity towards coffee and sweets transformed me into who I am and what I still like to this day. This is the privilege of family. I have been blessed with *familia* and with community.

*Recuerdos,* like *querencia*—a devotion, a seamlessness, a sense of safety, belonging transitioned into tradition, community, and always rooted in the landscape holding us.

My strength is from sunlight and rain. *Las golondrinas* (spring-time barn swallows) hurry across the sky, between green and blue, finding food for their young, finding *soquete* (mud) to build their nests. Impatient traffic is endless on the adjacent Highway 47, diesel trucks and piece-of-shit-cars alike. All of it at once, all of it within contradiction, yet still expanding, a *querencia* ethic expanding like the circles of community at the center of our culture, our lives radiating out in many directions, but it is our ties to family and community that bring us a sense of being and belonging.

Yet a land ethic rooted in *querencia* also understands the limits of our region's resources, and as Estévan Arellano states, "Sentiment and duty are not enough."[35]

So what will I teach my own boy, my own niece and nephew? What will I pass on of the wisdom shared with me? What will I offer within the actions of my own life?

*"When his son fell into a well, San Isidro didn't pray the deed undone, but asked for the water to rise—and the infant floated up into his arms."*

— LANCE LARSEN, *Aphorisms for a Lonely Planet* [37]

The Spanish-born saint, San Isidro, also known as *El Santo de la Tierra*, was said to have prayed diligently, so much so that angels were sent to his fields to finish his work so that he could continue to pray. He and his wife Maria had a son, and some accounts of the family detail how the young son fell into a well and was saved because of his parents' prayers. Other accounts tell how the child died young, his death propelling Isidro and Maria to become even more religiously devoted. It is said San Isidro was extremely pious and kind to animals.

Papa and San Isidro are both farmers, but only one is a saint. My Papa's tempers are quick but far between. He'll ask me to do something, but upon inspection, realize I didn't do it right, and has to do it correctly himself. Sometimes he curses. Most times he's worried. About rain when the hay is cut, about rain when grass is growing, about the actions of his son, about the mistakes of his daughter. Papa is a farmer but not yet a saint.

From the porch near the house, I see Papa in the distance, shovel on this shoulder. It is the outline of him as much as it is his presence, and I see him as an icon as much as a disciplined yet loving father. Egrets graze along the water that moves in and across the field, alfalfa fields lighting up the morning with a welcoming green. *Golondrinas* fly down and across the water, grasping at food too small for me to see or recognize. And Papa walks the field, slower with age, his boots soaking up the water, wearing them as the only lovely he knows.

*Querenica*—the place of your deepest identity, your deepest longing; a place in which we know exactly who we are; the place from which we speak our deepest beliefs.

## *Por Familia*
*Alamo Tree Looking onto My Father's Acequia*

# Afterword

Richard Rubin

This small Handbook was conceived among the environmental origins of Aldo Leopold's Land Ethic. Then we went forward from this past to describe present places and inspirational opportunities. Now we apply his advice for the future, that the Land Ethic evolves in the minds of a thinking community as a collective cultural effort. While it may seem that our ecological threats require predominately political and governmental solutions, scholars such as Ronald Brunner and Christine Colburn in their text *Finding Common Ground: Governance and Natural Resources in the American West* say:

> Environmental organizations clearly have begun to act on the wisdom of Aldo Leopold, whose classic statement of the land ethic still guides principled environmentalists. "To analyze the problem of action," Leopold wrote in 1942, "the first thing to grasp is that government, no matter how good, can only do certain things … . "

> Leopold suggested that we try self-government as a possible solution to problems of land abuse ... . " I refer rather to social and economic units who turn the light of self-scrutiny on themselves." Perhaps community-based initiatives are the self-scrutinizing units Leopold envisioned to propagate private ethics and naturalistic management, the things that most need doing.[38]

I share now my recognition of examples for future progress evident in early 2024, with apologies for not acknowledging all current worthy initiatives. Following our chapter topics, first we recognize that the influential skill inspired by Aldo's literature is fostered in the Albuquerque-based Leopold Writing Program among both school children and professional adults. Resident retreat opportunities at Mi Casita enhances their ecological muse inspiration. Next, we have many commentators and scholars producing texts and teaching opportunities that create growth and vitality. These may range from university classes to children's school programs. The programs at the Wisconsin-based Aldo Leopold Foundation provide training in land stewardship skills and educational leadership for the public. The continuing application of Phenology science is fostered by their calendar publication, expert commentaries by Senior Fellows, and presentations by prominent nature writers. They publish a school age curriculum guide called the Leopold Education Project.

Next, I applaud a new proposal advocating for Indigenous science research support that was published in the journal *Science* (January 19, 2024) by Robin Wall Kimmerer

## AFTERWORD

and Kyle Artelle of the Center for Native Peoples and the Environment at the State University of New York, Syracuse. They begin:

> Faced with the profound challenges of a rapidly changing environment, society needs other ways of knowing to illuminate a different way forward … . An urgent question is how institutions can appropriately support (and not hinder) Indigenous science's key role in creating a sustainable future … . For centuries, Indigenous scientists have had to adapt to, and develop fluency in, Western modes of knowledge making. It's now Western scientists' turn to learn from, and respect, Indigenous science (p. 243).

Following Leopold's challenge for humans to be citizens not conquerors of the land, international social justice issues are addressed by a United Kingdom on-line peer reviewed journal *Ecological Citizen* devoted to "Confronting human supremacy in defense of the Earth."

Future understanding of wilderness purpose and priorities is also expanding. Several University of New Mexico departments and programs are participating in the Centennial Ancestral Gila Homeland Project this year. Nongovernmental Organizations are providing boots-on-the-ground land ethic services and advocacy. New Mexico Wild publishes a comprehensive guide to New Mexico's protected wildlands and recruits youth for a Wilderness Ranger Program. The Rivers and Birds Program has worked for legal protection of several designated areas. The U.S. Forest Service conducts national Citizen Science Programs. Carson National Forest staff developed a Leopold Interpretive Trail extending from the Tres Piedras Ranger Station to Mosaic Rock and is formulating learning opportunities for school children there. The National Forest Foundation created the Nature Connects Us program "to spark awakening and strengthening of all peoples' connection to national forests and grasslands." The U.S. Department of Agriculture Working Lands for Wildlife program targets conservation efforts to improve agricultural and forest productivity which enhance wildlife habitat on working landscapes. The Albuquerque Wildlife Federation does vigorous public land restoration work such as the "check dams, gully plugging, and willow planting" Leopold advised for erosion control. These represent examples of Robin Wall Kimmerer's observation that repairing the wounds of the land also requires healing our ecological relationship. The nonprofit Freeflow Institute and Foundation provides young adults from marginalized communities with experiential education about writing in challenging western locations.

Ongoing responsibilities of private landowners are advanced from multiple sources. New Mexico State University is sponsoring an AgriVenture Symposium covering regenerative agriculture, soil health, wireless fencing, cattle outlooks, climate trends, and living with fire-prone landscapes. The Quivira Coalition based in Santa Fe pursues sustainable rangeland and ranching projects. The Alianza Agri-Cultura de Taos conducts small farm and ranch seminars. The Taos Land Trust Rio Fernando Park staff engage local school students in various organic gardens. The Taos chapter of the New Mexico Native Plant Society manages a greenhouse there and produces pollinator forbs for community distribution. The New Mexico Acequia Association conducts a Youth Leadership Institute , Con Fuerza y Querencia.

Coming back to our goal of seeking Land Ethic consciousness in ourselves, I add this articulate advice from Barry Lopez in his last book of essays, *Embrace Fearlessly the Burning World*:[39]

> If the first lesson in learning how to see more deeply into a landscape was to be continuously attentive, and to stifle the urge to stand *outside* the event, to instead stay *within* the event, leaving its significance to be resolved later, the second lesson, for me, was to notice how often I asked my body to defer to the dictates of my mind, how my body's extraordinary ability to discern textures and perfumes, to discriminate among tones and colors in the world outside itself, was dismissed by the rational mind. If we are true to Leopold's mandate for living in community, not commodification, this visceral wisdom is important.

# References

Aldington, Richard. *The Spirit of Place: An Anthology Compiled from the Prose of D.H. Lawrence.* Edited and with an Introduction by Richard Aldington. Readers Union, London, 1944.

Aldo Leopold Foundation. Exploring Your Land Ethic: Leopold Shack & Farm Self-Guided Tour. Aldo Leopold Foundation, 2023.

Allen, Elizabeth Hightower, editor. *First & Wildest: The Gila Wilderness at 100.* Torrey House Press, 2022.

Back, Joe. *Horses, Hitches, and Rocky Trails.* The Swallow Press, 1959.

Baden, John A and Snow, Donald, eds. *The Next West: Public Lands, Community, and Economy in the American West.* Island Press, 1997.

Berry, Wendell. *The Need To Be Whole: Patriotism and the History of Prejudice.* Shoemaker & Company, 2022.

Brookshier, Frank. *The Burro.* University of Oklahoma Press, 1974.

Brower, David R., ed. *Going Light With Backpack or Burro. Sierra Club.* Tenth printing 1968.

Brown, Cindy. *Taos Hiking Guide.* Nighthawk Press, 2015. second printing 2017.

Brown, David E. and Carmony, Neil B, eds. *Aldo Leopold's Southwest.* University of New Mexico Press, 1995.

Brunner, Ronald D., Christine H. Colburn, et al. *Finding Common Ground: Governance and Natural Resources in the American West.* Yale University Press, 2002.

Callicot, J. Baird, ed. *Companion to A Sand County Almanac.* The University of Wisconsin Press, 1987.

Carter, Jack. *Trees and Shrubs of New Mexico: Revised and Expanded.* Mimbres Publishing, 2012.

Cobos, Rubén. *A Dictionary of New Mexico and Southern Colorado Spanish.* Museum of New Mexico Press, 1983.

Connors, Philip. *Fire Season: Field Notes from a Wilderness Lookout.* Ecco Press, 2012.

deBuys, William and Harris, Alex. *River of Traps: A Village Life.* University of New Mexico Press, 1990.

Dombeck, Michael P.; Wood, Christopher A.; and Williams, Jack E. *From Conquest to Conservation: Our Public Lands Legacy.* Island Press, 2003.

Fairfax, Sally et al. *Buying Nature: The Limits of Land Acquisition as a Conservation Strategy, 1790–2004.* The MIT Press, 2005.

Flader, Susan L. *Thinking Like a Mountain: Aldo Leopold and the Evolution of an Ecological Attitude towards Deer, Wolves, and Forest.* University of Wisconsin Press, 1994.

Goldfarb, Ben. *Crossings: How Road Ecology is Shaping the Future of Our Planet.* W.W. Norton, 2023.

Gulliford, Andrew. *Sacred Objects and Sacred Places: Preserving Tribal Traditions.* University Press of Colorado, 2000.

Gulliford, Andrew, ed. *Preserving Western History.* University of New Mexico Press, 2005.

Gulliford, Andrew, ed. *Outdoors in the Southwest: An Adventure Anthology.* University of Oklahoma Press, 2014.

Carhart, Arthur H. and Young, Stanley. Andrew Gulliford and Tom Wolf, eds. *The Last Stand of the Pack: Critical Edition* by Arthur H. Carhart. University Press of Colorado, 2017.

Gulliford, Andrew. *The Woolly West: Colorado's Hidden History of Sheepscapes.* Texas A&M Press, 2018.

Huggard, Christopher J. and Gómez, Arthur R, eds. *Forests Under Fire: A Century of Ecosystem Mismanagement in the Southwest.* University of Arizona Press, 2001.

Kingsnorth, Paul. *Confessions of a Recovering Environmentalist and Other Essays.* Graywolf Press, 2017.

Larson, Lance. *Aphorisms for a Lonely Planet.* University of Tampa Press, 2017.

Laubach, Stephen A. *Living a Land Ethic: A History of Cooperative Conservation on the Leopold Memorial Reserve.* The University of Wisconsin Press, 2014.

# REFERENCES

Leopold, Aldo. *A Sand County Almanac and Sketches Here and There. Special 75th Anniversary Edition.* Introduction by Barbara Kingsolver, Oxford University Press, 2020.

Leopold, Estella B. *Stories from the Leopold Shack: Sand County Revisited.* Oxford University Press, 2016.

Leopold, Estella B. and Anderson, Alan. *Aldo's Wife Estella Bergere: My Remarkable Mother.* Aldo Leopold Foundation, 2022.

Lewis, Michael, ed. *American Wilderness: A New History.* Oxford University Press, 2007.

Loeffler, Jack and Loeffler, Celestia eds. *Thinking Like a Watershed*, University of New Mexico Press, 2012.

Lopez, Barry H. *Embrace Fearlessly the Burning World.* Random House, 2023.

Luong, Q.T. *Our National Monuments: America's Hidden Gems.* Terra Galleria Press, 2021.

Marshall, Peter. *Nature's Web: Rethinking Our Place on Earth.* Paragon House, 1994.

Meine, Curt. *Aldo Leopold: His Life and Works.* The University of Wisconsin Press, 1988.

Nash, Roderick. *Wilderness and the American Mind.* Yale University Press, 1967.

Pearce, T.M. *New Mexico Place Names: A Geographical Dictionary.* The University of New Mexico Press, 1965.

Robinson, Michael J. *Predatory Bureaucracy: The Extermination of Wolves and the Transformation of the West.* University Press of Colorado, 2005.

Rubin, Richard and Rubin, Annette. *Homescape Rewilding: Stories of Ordinary Ecological Practices.* Nighthawk Press, 2021.

Rubin, Richard. *Living the Leopolds' Mi Casita Ecology.* Nighthawk Press, 2022.

Rubin, Richard and Rubin, Annette. *Taos Horno Adventures: A Multicultural Culinary Memoir Informed by History and Horticulture.* Nighthawk Press, 2020.

Ruffin, Kimberly. *Black on Earth: African American Ecoliterary Traditions.* University of Georgia Press, 2010.

Salmon, M. H. *Home is the River.* High Lonesome Books, 1989.

Sanders, Scott Russell. *A Conservationist Manifesto.* Indiana University Press, 2009.

Sandler, Ronald and Cafaro, Philip, eds. *Environmental Virtue Ethics.* Rowman and Littlefield Publishers, 2005.

Ungnade, Herbert E. *Guide to the New Mexico Mountains.* University of New Mexico Press, 1965, sixth paperbound printing, 1983.

Wolf, Tom. *Arthur Carhart: Wilderness Prophet.* University Press of Colorado, 2008

Yong, Ed. *An Immense World: How Animal Senses Reveal the Hidden Realms Around Us.* Random House, 2023.

# NOTES (Andrew Gulliford)

## Foreword

1. See Gulliford, "Aldo Leopold, Estella Bergere, Mia Casita and Sheepherding in New Mexico and Colorado," *Natural Resources Journal,* published by the University of New Mexico School of Law, Vol. 57, No. 2, Summer 2017.

2. The definitive biography of Leopold is Curt Meine, *Aldo Leopold: His Life and Work* (Madison: University of Wisconsin Press, 1988).

3. This section of the foreword and a few other sections were first published in the author's monthly newspaper column "Gulliford's Travels" in the weekend edition of *The Durango* (Colorado) *Herald.*

4. Andrew Gulliford, *The Woolly West: Colorado's Hidden History of Sheepscapes* (College Station, Texas: Texas A&M University Press, 2018). The book won the Colorado Book Award in History and the Wrangler Award for Outstanding Non-Fiction from the National Cowboy & Heritage Museum in Oklahoma City.

5. The author is preparing a book length manuscript on the Bureau of Land Management's National Conservation Lands which include several sites in New Mexico such as the Rio Grande del Norte National Monument and others.

6. Estella B. Leopold, *Stories from the Leopold Shack: Sand County Revisited* (Madison: University of Wisconsin Press, 2016).

## Chapter 6

7. Thomas Wolf, *Arthur Carhart: Wilderness Prophet* (Boulder: University Press of Colorado, 2008).

8. For the failure of Mexican wolf re-introduction see articles in *High Country News* and Michael J. Robinson, *Predatory Bureaucracy: The Extermination of Wolves and the Transformation of the West* (Boulder: University Press of Colorado, 2005). For a novel about introducing Mexican wolves see M. H. "Dutch" Salmon, *Home is the River* (Silver City, New Mexico: High Lonesome Books, 1989).

9. For an earlier version of this essay see Andrew Gulliford, "Geronimo, Aldo and Earth First! All Basked in the Nation's

First Wilderness Area," *Trilogy Magazine*, May/June 1991. Also see Christopher J. Huggard, "America's First Wilderness Area," in Christopher J. Huggard and Arthur R. Gomez, eds., *Forests Under Fire* (Tucson: University of Arizona Press, 2001).

10. Gulliford, "Geronimo, Aldo, and Earth First!"

11. In the spirit of Aldo Leopold, legislation to protect the Gila, San Francisco, and East Fork of the Mimbres Rivers under the Wild and Scenic River Act is going forward as the M.H. Dutch Salmon Greater Gila Wild and Scenic River Act. New Mexico Wild proclaims, "This bill honors the original vision of Aldo Leopold and river champions like the late Dutch Salmon, without whose efforts this river we love would have been greatly diminished."

12. For an excellent overview of the 1964 Wilderness Act and the compromises involved in its legislative passage see Steven C. Schulte, "Where Man is a Visitor: The Wilderness Act as a Case Study in Public History," in Andrew Gulliford, ed. *Preserving Western History* (Albuquerque: University of New Mexico Press, 2005). For an overview of wilderness perspectives in America the classic reference is Roderick Nash, *Wilderness and the American Mind* Fourth Edition. New Haven, Conn.: Yale University Press, 2001). Also see Michael Lewis, ed. *American Wilderness: A New History* (New York: Oxford University Press, 2007).

13. To understand the impacts of the 1910 fire and subsequent fire suppression see Timothy Egan, *The Big Burn: Teddy Roosevelt and the Fire That Saved America* (Boston: Houghton Mifflin, 2009).

14. To learn more see Philip Connors, *Fire Season* (Ecco Press, 2012).

15. See Andrew Gulliford, *Sacred Objects and Sacred Places: Preserving Tribal Traditions* (Boulder: University Press of Colorado, 2000). Also see Gulliford, "The Pothunting Problem: Thieves of Times in the American West," *Utah Adventure Journal*, May 12, 2017.

16. See Howard L. Smith, "The Gila Wilderness—Southwestern New Mexico," in Andrew Gulliford, ed. *Outdoors in the Southwest: An Adventure Anthology* (Norman: University of Oklahoma Press, 2014).

## Chapter 7

17. Andrew Gulliford and Tom Wolf, eds. *The Last Stand of the Pack: Critical Edition* (Boulder: University Press of Colorado, 2017). Some of the writing in this essay is excerpted from the book and from newspaper columns the author has written for the *Durango Herald* and *High Country News*.

18. See M.J. Robinson, *Predatory Bureaucracy: The Extermination of Wolves and the Transformation of the West* (Boulder: University Press of Colorado, 2005).

19. Colorado Parks & Wildlife, *CPW News Release—Moffat County Wolves,* November 23, 2020.

20. Carhart letter cited in Robinson, *Predatory Bureaucracy,* 222-223.

21. Interview on horseback with Dan Schwartz, owner and outfitter at Ripple Creek Lodge, Rio Blanco County, September 18, 2015.

22. Susan L. Flader, *Thinking Like A Mountain: Aldo Leopold and the Evolution of an Ecological Attitude toward Deer, Wolves and Forest* (Madison: University of Wisconsin Press, 1994).

23. Gary Skiba, personal communication with author, December 26, 2020. Also see Andrew Gulliford "Learning to Live with Wolves Again in Colorado," *Waving Hands Review: Literature and Art of Northwest Colorado,* Vol. 13, Issue 13, 2021.

# NOTES (Richard Rubin and Leeanna Torres)

## Introduction

1. Aldo Leopold, *A Sand County Almanac and Sketches Here and There* (New York: Oxford University Press, 2020), p.212. This is a 75th anniversary paperback edition of the original published in 1949.

2. www.aldoleopold.org

3. Curt Meine, *Aldo Leopold: His Life and Works* (Madison: The University of Wisconsin Press, 1988), p. 329.

4. Friends of Mi Casita Fund, taoscf.org.

5. abqwildlifefederation.org, founded by Leopold in 1914.

## Chapter 1

6. Op. cit., Introduction by Barbara Kingsolver. P. xx.

7. Kimberly Ruffin, *Black on Earth: African American Ecoliterary Traditions* (Athens: University of Georgia Press, 2010).

## Chapter 2

8. For an earlier and more extensive version on this topic, see Richard and Annette Rubin, *Homescape Rewilding: Stories of Ordinary Ecological Practices* (Taos: Nighthawk Press, 2021), p.xix–xxi.

9. J. Baird Callicott, editor, *Companion to A Sand County Almanac* (Madison: University of Wisconsin Press, 1987), Appendix p. 282.

10. *A Sand County Almanac,* Op. cit. p.191.

11. Peter Marshall, *Nature's Web: Rethinking our Place on Earth* (New York: Paragon House, 1994. p. 356).

12. The Leopold Writing Program, www.leopoldwritingprogram.org, provides month long scholarship retreats at Mi Casita.

13. Ben Goldfarb, *Crossings: How Road Ecology is Shaping the Future of our Planet* (New York: W.W. Norton 2023).

14. Ronald Sandler and Philip Cafarro editors, *Environmental Virtue Ethics* (Lanham Maryland, Rowman and Littlefield, 2005)

15. Curt Meine and Nina Leopold Bradley, "The Once and Future Land Ethic," in *From Conquest to Conservation: Our Public Lands Legacy* (Washington D.C.: Island Press, 2003.

16. Wendell Berry, *The Need To Be Whole: Patriotism and the History of Prejudice* (New York: Shoemaker & Company, 2022).

## Chapter 3

17. This memoir was published privately by the Aldo Leopold Foundation and personally received on my request from Executive Director Buddy Huffaker.

18. Sally Fairfax et al. *Buying Nature: The Limits of Land Acquisition as a Conservation Strategy, 1790–2004* (Cambridge: The MIT Press, 2005).

19. Mawr comes from Welsh meaning large or great. The name refers specifically to a magnificent horse Lawrence saw in Wales, not New Mexico, and made a character in the novella.

20. The house building foreman was Walter Perry, and he is credited with constructing this fireplace from native volcanic rocks following Leopold's directions. The Mi Casita library includes his memoir edited by Les Joslin, *Walter Perry: An Early-Day Forest Ranger in New Mexico and Oregon* (Wilderness Associates, 1999).

21. David E. Brown & Neil B. Carmony, editors, *Aldo Leopold's Southwest* (Albuquerque, University of New Mexico Press, 1990).

22. Aldo Leopold, *Game Management* (Madison: University of Wisconsin Press, 1933).

## Chapter 4

23. More extensive description of the history, setting, construction, Forest Service use, National Historic Registration, 2005–6 Restoration, and subsequent programs at Mi Casita can be found in Richard Rubin, *Living the Leopolds' Mi Casita Ecology* (Taos: Nighthawk Press, 2022). Foreword by Curt Meine and photographs curated by Annette Rubin.

24. Personal communication, 2024.

## Chapter 5

25. Aldo Leopold, "The Wilderness and Its Place in Forest Recreation Policy," *Journal of Forestry,* November, 1921.

26. Elizabeth Hightower Allen, editor, *First and Wildest: The Gila Wilderness at 100* (Salt Lake City: Torrey House Press, 2022).

27. Roderick Nash, *Wilderness and the American Mind* (New Haven: Yale University Press, 1967).

28. Aldo Leopold, "Wilderness Values" in *Living Wilderness,* 7, (1942).

29. Herbert Unguade, *A Guide to the New Mexico Mountains* (Albuquerque: University of New Mexico Press, second edition, 1972).

30. Cindy Brown, *Taos Hiking Guide* (Taos, Nighthawk Press, 2017).

31. www.wilderness.org/articles/article/national-wilderness-preservation-system

32. Scott Russell Sanders, *A Conservation Manifesto* (Bloomington: Indiana University Press, 2009).

## Chapter 9

33. QT Luong, *Our National Monuments: America's Hidden Gems* (San Jose, CA, Terra Galleria Press, 2021. I am grateful for a signed copy given by the Rivers and Birds Board for my philanthropy).

34. Roberta Salazar, Arroyo Seco NM, personal communication 2024.

## Chapter 10

35. Juan Estevan Arellano, *La Cuenca y la Querencia: The Watershed and the Sense of Place in the Merced and Acequia Landscape*. In Jack and Celestia Loeffler eds, *Thinking Like a Watershed*. (University of New Mexico Press, 2012) p.151-152.

36. See https://culture.wnmu.edu/events/recuerdos

37. Lance Larson, *Aphorisms for a Lonely Planet* (Tampa: University of Tampa Press, 2017).

## Afterword

38. Ronald Brunner and Christine Colburn, *Find Common Ground: Governance and Natural Resources in the American West* (New Haven: Yale University Press, 2002) p.229-230.

39. Barry Lopez, *Embrace Fearlessly the Burning World* (New York: Random House, 2023) p.68.

www.ingramcontent.com/pod-product-compliance
Lightning Source LLC
Chambersburg PA
CBHW052030030426
42337CB00027B/4937